creating a
digital-rich
classroom

Teaching & Learning in a Web 2.0 World

Meg Ormiston

Solution Tree | Press

a division of

Solution Tree

555 North Morton Street
Bloomington, IN 47404
800.733.6786 (toll free) / 812.336.7700
FAX: 812.336.7790

email: info@solution-tree.com
solution-tree.com

Visit **go.solution-tree.com/technology** for links to the websites in this book.

Printed in the United States of America

14 13 12 11 10   1 2 3 4 5

FSC
Mixed Sources
Product group from well-managed
forests and other controlled sources

Cert no. SW-COC-002283
www.fsc.org
© 1996 Forest Stewardship Council

Library of Congress Cataloging-in-Publication Data

Ormiston, Meghan J.
  Creating a digital-rich classroom : teaching & learning in a web 2.0 world / Meg Ormiston.
       p. cm.
  Includes bibliographical references and index.
  ISBN 978-1-935249-88-7 (library binding) -- ISBN 978-1-935249-87-0 (perfect bound) 1. Internet in education. 2. Internet searching--Study and teaching. 3. Web 2.0. 4. Electronic information resource literacy--Study and teaching. I. Title.
  LB1044.87.O76 2011
  371.33'44678--dc22
                                        2010025193

Solution Tree
Jeffrey C. Jones, CEO & President

Solution Tree Press
President: Douglas M. Rife
Publisher: Robert D. Clouse
Vice President of Production: Gretchen Knapp
Managing Production Editor: Caroline Wise
Senior Production Editor: Lesley Bolton
Proofreader: Elisabeth Abrams
Cover and Text Designer: Amy Shock

This book is dedicated to educators at all levels who work tirelessly
to make a difference in the lives of children; to my first teacher,
my mom, Marta, who is an inspiration to us all; to my talented
team of assistants, Lauren and Laurie, without whose help this
book would still be in outline form; and to those at home, my
husband, Brian, and my young men, Danny and Patrick,
who teach me something new every day and who help me
stay grounded and focused on how learning
really needs to be about engagement.

Acknowledgments

Solution Tree Press would like to thank the following reviewers:

Lindsay Cesari
Library Media Specialist
Durgee Junior High
Baldwinsville, New York

Howie DiBlasi
Consultant
Digital Journey
Georgetown, Texas

Christopher Moersch
Executive Director
LoTi Connection, Inc.
Carlsbad, California

Cindy Moore
English Teacher
Dodge City High School
Fort Dodge, Kansas

Mike Musil
English Teacher
North Star High School
Lincoln, Nebraska

Laurence Peters
Adjunct Professor, Graduate
School of Management and
Technology
University of Maryland
University College
Adelphi, Maryland

Bernajean Porter
Education Technology
Consultant
Bernajean Porter Consulting
Denver, Colorado

Kathy Schrock
Director of Technology
Nauset Public Schools
Orleans, Massachusetts

Visit **go.solution-tree.com/technology** for links to the websites in this book.

Table of Contents

About the Author

For over twenty-five years, Meg Ormiston has been involved in professional development activities focused on changing instructional practice in the classroom. Meg marries her passion for technology with a deep curriculum background and over twelve years' experience as a classroom teacher having taught several grade levels and served as a math coach and a technology coach for K–8.

Meg has served as a curriculum coach, school board member, internationally known keynote speaker, professional development specialist, and grant facilitation specialist. Meg has authored two books, written numerous articles, and collaborated on professional videos. She also participates in many personal learning communities.

Meg holds a master's degree in curriculum and instruction and uses current research and practical methods to help educators improve teaching and learning in their classrooms.

It's a Web 2.0 World

Learning is all about engagement. As e-learning guru Roger C. Schank (2002) says, "First and foremost: When learning isn't engaging, it's not learning" (p. 10). Today's classrooms are at the center of a revolution that has technology at its core. The ever-expanding array of technological tools for communication and collaboration are cultural currency, part of a social growth engine that is defining how everyone—regardless of age or economic circumstances—interacts with people and ideas. Districts, schools, and teachers must realize that failure to make new technology integral to teaching and learning will render them irrelevant to students.

Web 2.0—a term that is rapidly becoming overused—also is known as the "Read/Write Web." The term *Web 2.0* is associated with applications that promote collaboration. Many Web 2.0 sites are blocked behind firewalls because they are designed for this interactivity. Social networking sites are just one subgroup of Web 2.0. Others include live video streaming, blogging, podcasts, and wikis, all of which will be discussed in this book. Driven by Internet technology, Web 2.0 is defined by its capacity for and reliance on active participation by Internet users.

Originally, webpages were written and posted, and then many of them faded like old bulletin boards. Rarely updated, the content became stale, and viewers stopped using the pages as resources. Today, web tools are designed for collaboration and require continual updating. People try out sites and see how they work. The good sites stick around, while the others fade away.

This dynamic environment makes for an exciting time in education. Teachers can try out many forms of technology—hardware, software, websites—and choose the best among them to integrate into their classrooms. The future of education is here today. I see big changes and big challenges, both of which will be explored in this book. But the bottom line is this: when the collaborative Web 2.0 tools that are described in this book are made a part of the teaching and learning process, they bring the entire world to the classroom in ways never before possible.

Why This Book, and Why Now

The purpose of this book is to provide a research base and practical strategies to help teachers design and deliver lessons in which technology plays an integral role. It isn't simply a matter of schools spending money to buy digital tools (or "toys," as some critics would have it). The essential idea is that engaging students in solving real-world problems of today and tomorrow means using the technological tools that are shaping our world and using them in a meaningful way.

Web 2.0 tools bring amazing potential to teaching and learning. For instance, students can link to teachers and classmates within their own school, but they also can connect beyond the school—to online organizations, to institutions with an Internet presence, and to other schools. These outside connections can be as close as across town or as distant as the other side of the world.

Engagement is necessary for acquiring knowledge and applying new understandings to solve real problems. Technology is not causing this engagement; restructured learning is. Of course, anytime new tools and structures become available, there are those who throw up roadblocks to change. We—educators, administrators, parents— must roll up our sleeves, tear down those barriers, and really focus on what is important about teaching and learning today.

This book is not for my friends in the educational technology world; they are already aware of the benefits of Web 2.0 tools. Instead, it is for all the other educators out there. My hope is that this book reaches teachers at all levels who are interested in engaging students through authentic learning. Authentic learning mirrors the tasks and problem solving that are required in the reality outside of school. More often than not in the modern world, the ways to collaborate and communicate rely on technology. Regardless of grade level or content specialty, whether techie or newbie, teachers will find that this book offers ideas to refocus teaching and to engage students in active learning in new, exciting ways. The content is not only pertinent for teachers already in the field but also will be useful to teacher educators and preservice teachers.

Integrated Technology

The days are long gone when technology was a class and students only used computers in the computer lab down the hall. Today every professional educator needs to be using technology with students every day. The current generation of learners craves technology; multiple media are woven into the fabric of their personal lives. Our standards-aligned curricula can be enhanced with powerful technological resources to transform and enrich content—and make it more accessible and relevant to students. We now need a sense of urgency to get the technological tools and resources into classrooms that can make substantial improvements in students' learning.

A clear focus on engagement must drive this transformation. All the technological bells and whistles in the world will not engage students unless teachers structure meaningful learning situations. This book offers guidance for accomplishing such change. Differentiated instruction expert Carol Tomlinson (1999a) wrote, "Lessons that are not engaging let students' minds wander. They fail to make the case for relevance because students don't connect them to what's important in their lives. These kinds of lessons have little staying power. Thus, the learner has little long-term use for un-engaging lessons" (p. 38). We will explore a variety of topics related to engaging students with and through technology.

Chapter Summaries

Looking at the classrooms of today is the focus of chapter 1, starting with how today's students are very different because they are so connected and technology is pervasive in their lives. Examining how different their world is outside of the classroom leads to the discussion about roadblocks to making change in the classroom. The teacher plays a pivotal role in a transformed classroom if true change is to be sustained.

Engaged students and teachers are not always quiet. Students are not all sitting in their seats, doing the same thing. Active engagement can look messy to an outside observer. Yet, if structured correctly, this type of classroom can be an extraordinarily rich learning environment. In chapter 2, I examine how planning for active learning differs from planning a "stand and deliver," textbook-driven lesson. True active learning is the ultimate in differentiated instruction, with the teacher learning and exploring alongside students. Also, active learning is not bounded by classroom walls but carries over to what students do outside the formal school setting to continue engaging with ideas and their applications in the real world.

Technology can be overwhelming, and using it ineffectively can be detrimental to fundamental aspects of teaching and learning. Therefore, in chapter 3, I concentrate on dealing not only with the technological tools but also with how highly engaged teachers and learners can best use technology in meaningful ways—beyond the bells and whistles. Engagement increases when learners have options for *how* they are going to learn. Everyone has likes and dislikes, strengths and weaknesses, and so options are important. Differentiation and active learning are intertwined, and time and effort must be dedicated to collaboration. Tomlinson (1999b) pointed out, "In differentiated classrooms, teachers begin [teaching] where students are, not at the front of the curriculum guide" (p. 2).

Outfitting classrooms with technology does not automatically transform a passive classroom into one of high engagement. Lessons need to be defined or redefined, and substantive changes are crucial. Using technological tools correctly brings the world into the classroom and opens up amazing possibilities. Yet there are obstacles, such as budgetary constraints, lack of leadership, ineffective professional development, and other issues (or excuses!). These obstacles can be overcome if a focus is maintained on the need for active engagement as a means to increase student achievement.

In chapter 4, I demonstrate the possibilities for active engagement when digital resources are integral to the curriculum. The examples include high-tech but not necessarily high-priced technological tools, such as streaming media, virtual field trips, and resources that teachers can use to connect their classrooms, literally, to the world.

In chapter 5, I explore the technological tools no classroom should be without. Of course, policies and standards come into play with this consideration. Some educators fear that students will encounter inappropriate material when using the Internet in school. The reality is that students go home to unfiltered high-speed networks and unmonitored cell phones, often without having acquired the skills for appropriate use. The National Educational Technology Standards (NETS) specifically detail the skills that schools should be teaching so that students become responsible digital citizens.

In chapter 6, we will take a virtual field trip to a restructured fifth-grade classroom. This trip will help you better visualize the possibilities for a restructured classroom utilizing Web 2.0 tools. I focus on the students' on-task behavior, general digital resources, the roles of the teacher and administrator, feedback from parents, and the specific Web 2.0 tools used in this active-learning classroom.

In chapter 7, I introduce personal learning networks as valuable resources for professional development. You already have personal learning networks with colleagues at school and within your district. Some of you are fortunate to have opportunities to network beyond your locale by attending regional or national conferences. Some of you also may be involved in graduate studies, which creates another professional network. Beyond these face-to-face connections, however, lie a vast number of networking opportunities literally at your fingertips thanks to the digital world. The collaborative Web 2.0 tools available today provide instant access to distant colleagues and information, allowing educators everywhere to expand their reach across the country or around the globe. Tapping this potential in many cases will require a shift in thinking, not only about networking as a way of taking personal responsibility for professional growth, but also about how best to accomplish such networking.

The goal of the epilogue is to look forward and create an implementation plan that will make active learning possible. This new approach to teaching and learning will require curriculum changes to incorporate the collaborative possibilities. There is a focus in the epilogue on making professional development personal and on continued learning with Web 2.0 tools.

Finally, I include an appendix that provides a compendium of the Web 2.0 tools touched on throughout this book as well as a few others that may be helpful to teachers and students. The compendium is organized into use categories to serve as a ready reference. Visit **go.solution-tree.com/technology** for links to the websites in this book.

Getting Started

Each summer for almost a decade, I have served as an adjunct professor, teaching technology-immersion classes for a local university. These classes have become more sophisticated as the technological tools have evolved. These intense, graduate-level classes prepare practicing teachers to use Web 2.0 tools in their own classrooms and challenge them to redesign their lessons. At these "tech camps," I am continually amazed by the creativity, complexity, and variety of the digital stories that teachers create as part of their work with previously unfamiliar technological tools. (Digital storytelling marries multimedia with the art of storytelling.) These classes provide starting points for change, innovation, and for many students, renewal.

This book also offers starting points for those of you willing to embark on a journey toward the new era in education. Outside of school, today's students are accustomed to a high level of interaction and collaboration—with one another and with technology. We cannot continue to ask these students to "power down" and disconnect from their world, assuming that we can help them achieve their fullest potential through traditional methods.

Teachers at all levels need permission—as much from themselves as from their supervisors—to learn, play, collaborate, and experiment with Web 2.0 tools. They need to immerse themselves in unfamiliar technology through active participation in social-professional networks of all kinds, as well as through their own exploration.

The future is here, and our students are way ahead of us. I hope that you will use this book as a starting point to create new learning opportunities that will capture students emotionally and help them connect with the curriculum in new ways made possible by today's technology.

chapter 1

Today's Classrooms

Dreams of making a difference and creating a better future for students brought most of us into the field of education. Many of us *are* making a difference in the lives of the children we teach, but in my opinion, we do not teach in the ways that our students learn best. Learning today is an entirely new game.

New technology offers possibilities for increased student engagement, yet without a change in planning and delivery of instruction, there will not be a significant increase in student achievement. Our instructional and classroom management methods need to be brought up to date, and we need to be retrained.

Retraining does occur in most school districts, but it is often focused on a new reading series or hands-on science program. The retraining I envision is not specific to a curricular area; instead, it is more global, looking at the process of teaching in a more engaging way.

Students Today Are Different

Many Web 2.0 tools come naturally to today's students; they have never known a world in which such things did not exist. Cognitive scientists are conducting some compelling research, detailing exactly why today's students are so different from students a mere decade ago.

In his book *iBrain: Surviving the Technological Alteration of the Modern Mind*, neuroscientist Gary Small (Small & Vorgan, 2008) explains,

> Daily exposure to high technology—computers, smart phones, video games, search engines like Google and Yahoo—stimulates brain cell alteration

and neurotransmitter release, gradually strengthen-
ing new neural pathways in our brains while weaken-
ing old ones. Because of the current technological
revolution, our brains are evolving right now—at a
speed like never before. (p. 1)

Let's look at current high school freshmen. As I write this book,
these ninth-graders are youngsters who were born in the first half
of the 1990s. They have never lived without the Internet. When
they were babies, they probably heard screechy modems whenever their parents started surfing the mostly text-based World Wide
Web of that period. But by kindergarten, many of their homes and
schools already had relatively fast Internet connections. Certainly,
the turn of the new century ushered in widespread availability of
high-speed Internet connectivity.

In fact, this freshman class is older than many of today's Internet
company giants. The freshman group automatically turns to
Google or YouTube, when previous generations would have
headed to the library, opened a phone book, or consulted an encyclopedia. A January 2010 Kaiser Family Foundation study, titled
Generation M: Media in the Lives of 8- to 18-Year-Olds, reported that
"eight- to eighteen-year-olds spend more time with media than
any other activity besides (maybe) sleeping—an average of more
than 7½ hours a day, seven days a week" (Rideout, Foehr, &
Roberts, 2010, p. 1).

Many of these ninth-graders have been connecting with one
another by cell phone since early middle school. Text messaging,

Well-Known Sites and Their Start Dates

eBay 1995

Amazon.com 1995

Yahoo! 1995

Google 1998

Wikipedia 2001

Facebook 2004

YouTube 2005

or texting, has given them a whole new language and a new way to communicate, making the spoken phone call almost obsolete—at least from peers; parents still insist on calling. Texting has become a communication mainstay for these students, while many adults are still challenged by the older technology of email.

Most cell phones today are mini-computers that can be individualized in a wide variety of ways. Some high-performance, or "smart," phones allow users to download applications (apps), or small software programs that range from highly customized applications for business, education, and travel to fun apps such as games. Hundreds of thousands of these apps are available. Many are available free or for a minimal charge to download from the Internet, and all are designed to allow each cell phone user to create a custom experience. Our freshmen are more conversant with the latest apps than most adults can ever hope to be.

At these students' age, many of their parents were watching television that offered only a handful of channels, and they were getting up to turn the volume and channel-selection knobs. Today's television sets more often than not are connected to a cable or satellite service. The lineup of channels—accessed at the touch of a button on a remote—seems nearly infinite and is supplemented by "on demand" channels. Television programs also can now be watched on computers or mobile devices, all using the Internet. The advent of new technologies has provided seemingly endless choices and therefore the ability to truly individualize one's experience.

Immersed in video and computer games since they were toddlers, our freshmen have been "bathed in bits," as Don Tapscott (2009, p. 39) observes in his book *Grown Up Digital: How the Net Generation Is Changing Your World*. Manipulating objects, solving complex problems, and collaborating with others during the process are what they know. As they have grown, so has the sophistication of the games they play. The complexity of many video games and the collaboration it takes to be successful at them are not as easily understood by adults as they are by these ninth-graders. Often, it is a humbling experience for parents who try to compete against one of these successful gamers. Youthful gamers also learn a complex vocabulary and a wealth of strategies for manipulating the games.

It is not uncommon for groups of gamers to gather and learn from one another, exploring games, strategies, and websites—precisely the kind of collaboration that also can activate classroom learning.

> I happen to live with a proud member of this freshman class. I distinctly remember Danny racing off the bus one day after kindergarten, excited to share what he experienced in music class. He said something like, "Mom, you won't believe this! Mrs. Z had this thing today, it looked like a CD, but it was bigger and it was black. She put it on this machine that spins, and she put a needle on it, and music came out. It was so cool! Have you ever seen anything like that?" Danny was a little crestfallen when I took him downstairs and showed him his dad's record collection and the turntable he still uses.

Many of us of an age to be parents of these ninth-graders have collected music since our own teen years. Remember the crates of record albums and singles, then eight-track tapes, later cassettes, and finally CDs? Compact discs, or CDs, have been around since the 1980s—they are what our freshmen have always used to play music. But even CDs soon, if not already, may seem dated to these ninth-graders. With the advent of mp3 players and iPods, they have been downloading music from the Internet. Gone are the days of buying a whole album for one or two songs. Now, we can purchase our favorite music song by song. These songs can then be imported into a computer-based library, organized into playlists, and burned to a custom CD or downloaded to a portable listening device, including a cell phone.

The same kinds of transitions have occurred with video material. Remember the debate over which technology was best, BETA or VHS? VHS won out only to be rendered obsolete by the advent of DVDs. And now there's Blu-ray. Our ninth-graders have always known DVDs, but now they also can download videos from the Internet and play them on their computers, portable DVD players, iPods, and cell phones. Again, today's consumer can customize his or her technology in a seemingly infinite variety of ways.

Understanding the concept of customization is critical to understanding this new generation and the ones right behind it. Our freshmen customize their television viewing, video watching, game playing, music listening, and even with whom and how they connect online or by phone. Many, if not most, of these students' teachers grew up in a very different world, one in which the capacity to customize technology was limited—and, indeed, in many cases where technology itself was the merest foreshadowing of today's digital landscape.

According to the Kaiser Family Foundation study cited previously, "Today the typical 8- to 18-year-old's home contains an average of 3.8 TVs, 2.8 DVD or VCR players, 1 digital video recorder, 2.2 CD players, 2.5 radios, 2 computers, and 2.3 console video game players" (Rideout, Foehr, & Roberts, 2010, p. 9). Researchers found that 93 percent of these homes have at least one home computer. Most, though not all, homes have the technology commonly used by our freshmen. However, when such technology is not available, problems can arise in terms of learning as well as social acceptability. Often it falls to schools to fill in the gaps, which can present financial and logistical challenges.

Power Down and Come to School

Now, what happens when these young people—who, outside of school, are connected, collaborative, and creative—come to school?

The fast-paced whirl of media is stilled in the classroom. Students are expected to sit, listen, and take notes verbatim while teachers lecture or write on the board for most of the period. Teachers are the ones doing the work in many classrooms, and "successful" students are those who can sit still and "play school." Students who do not master the game of school do not succeed, and in fact, such students are dropping out in record numbers. Dropouts frequently cite boredom as the main reason for their decision to leave school before graduation. Research indicates that "both academic and social engagement are integral components of successfully navigating the education pipeline" and that "a lack of student engagement is predictive of dropping out, even after controlling for academic achievement and student background" (Rumberger, 2004).

Sadly, our school culture can actually breed complacency. Many educators are content to just dust off the same activities they have always employed and do only what it takes to get by. Some staff members attend workshops on new initiatives but never implement them. There is little urgency for engaging students, little urgency for change.

Of course, this is not the case everywhere, but even one classroom in one school is too many! We must light a fire under every educator, administrator, school board member, politician, parent, and community member because, in the end, if we are not engaging kids, we are not doing our job.

Roadblocks to Change

Our schools are resistant to change. Departments in most central offices compete against each other for precious resources. Rarely, technology and curriculum come together, though technological tools can support every subject area.

Often budgets become the excuse for impeding change. School funding is impacted by so many variables that it is often hard to plan ahead for purchasing new and replacement equipment. We must rethink allocations and employ creative problem solving. Funding for technology will be available when it becomes a priority, but this can only happen when departments collaborate with a singular focus on student engagement.

Many districts make these technology changes incrementally. They create a classroom standard for equipment, and as funds become available, they roll out the equipment to the next group of teachers.

Leadership is critical to the budgeting process. School administrators must advocate for change. In my experience, schools that make the biggest changes in culture and use of technology usually have an administrator who advocates for technology and models the use of it daily.

It is important to educate the school board about the need for technology in the process of teaching and learning. As a former school board member, I participated in field trips to neighboring districts to see the technology being used in classrooms. I also met with board members from those districts to talk about how they budgeted and planned for the initiative. School board members find it helpful to attend conferences that showcase the latest in technology. They can then take back what they learned to the board.

Be a Hero

The professional educators who are completely focused on engaging students and are willing to take risks and try new methods are heroes to the educational system. These heroes are not just the new teachers who are fresh out of school and armed with youthful idealism and energy. Many of our veteran teachers are leading the innovation, reinventing themselves and how they present information. Unfortunately, because of limited school budgets, there are many heroes waiting for their chance to shine.

Be a hero. Use your creativity to get past the roadblocks. Apply for grants. The process can often be laborious, but sometimes it can be as simple as filling out an online form. Because we do have financial constraints, creativity is crucial, so leverage the power of your online community to solicit ideas about funding. When trying to secure equipment, I've found it effective to lead with, "I can help my students be more successful in this area [be specific] if I had these tools."

Continue to grow and nurture relationships with your colleagues by sharing what you are learning through your networks. Attend workshops and conferences and model the use of technology in your school. Think about creating a professional learning community within the school that supports a bank of ideas and resources for everyone to access.

First Steps

When I look to the future, I see classrooms in which every learner will be connected to every other learner through digital tools. Learning will expand, extending the possibilities beyond the walls of the school. The roles of the teacher and learner will shift; the teacher will learn alongside the student, and the student will be in charge of his or her learning, setting goals and creating a plan to reach those goals. Digital resources will be employed to design the curriculum. Technology will help create a learning environment

that deeply engages the students in constant reflection, conversation, and redesign.

All of this is possible today. The tools are ready, or in development.
The challenge is to break down the barriers and change the culture
of our schools. The students are ready; they crave engagement.
According to Tomlinson (1999a),

> Engagement happens when a lesson captures stu-
> dents' imaginations, snares their curiosity, ignites
> their opinions, or taps into their souls. Engagement
> is the magnet that attracts learners' meandering
> attention and holds it so that enduring learning can
> occur. Understanding means much more than recall-
> ing. It means the learner has "wrapped around" an
> important idea, has incorporated it accurately into
> his or her inventory of how things work. The learner
> owns the idea. (p. 38)

I believe in this transcendent future. But how do we get there?

A first step in this transformation will be for teachers, administrators, and policymakers to examine policies and procedures concerning students' access to and use of technology such as cell
phones and websites. What policies must be changed in order to
integrate Web 2.0 meaningfully in lessons? What personal technology might students be permitted to use in schools for educational purposes?

For example, many cell phone policies were written before the
advent of smartphones, or even phones equipped with built-in
cameras. Later in this book, I will delve deeper into the debate
about cell phone use in schools, but it is important to understand at the outset that cell phones possess potential for enhancing and extending learning, in large measure because students are
so familiar with them and use them with ease and frequency. Most
older cell phone policies ignore the potential for using cell phones
educationally, for instance, to enable one-to-one computing.

Many districts also block and filter many of the Web 2.0 tools
because they are considered social networking sites. To be compli-
ant with the federal Children's Internet Protection Act (CIPA), districts do need to filter sites, but many districts are blocking websites

that could be used for teaching and learning. There needs to be systems in place to unblock websites to be used with students.

Policies that dwell on only the negative potential of technology ignore the enormous positive potential for authentic learning. We can either keep doing what we are doing or try something new. Our students are bored with traditional methods of instruction. This book is about what we can do differently. By leveraging new resources, tools, policies, and teaching methods, it is possible to truly engage our students in authentic learning. The upcoming chapters will provide an in-depth look at strategies for engagement utilizing technology.

chapter 2

Active Learning in the Classroom

Active learning is when students are completely engaged in challenging and authentic learning activities. When actively learning, students are self-motivated to complete demanding tasks that hold their attention, and seamless and ongoing classroom assessment helps them to self-regulate their learning.

The active-learning classroom today is an environment in which technology—much of it involving Web 2.0—is integral. A significant amount of active learning also is likely to be collaborative, depending on the task or activity, and the learning activities may continue outside the school day, using Web 2.0 tools to extend the face-to-face collaboration of the classroom. However, the focus in active learning—whether in the classroom or elsewhere, whether individual or collaborative—cannot be merely on hardware and software. Instead, the focus must be engagement, the critical element that makes learning truly "active."

Lack of engagement is a central problem in education. According to Michael Furdyk, cofounder of an online community for youth interested in global issues, TakingITGlobal, much of this problem results from a lack of engaging content:

> "Everything else has become so engaging," says Furdyk. "N-geners who go online regularly to play video games or interact on MySpace expect better experiences in the classroom. Look at today's curriculum, though, and you won't find much interactivity. We're still learning through reading and regurgitating." (Tapscott & Williams, 2006, p. 51)

One solution to the engagement problem involves incorporating appropriate technological tools in instruction to foster and facilitate active learning. Many such tools are available, and the best among them support and encourage collaborative learning. Collaborative learning mirrors students' innate desire for connection not only with interesting, relevant content but also with other students. Depending on the learning activity, such technological tools can include anything from cell phones to webcam communications through Skype to computer-based academic chats and interactive e-classrooms in which students share learning activities with peers in other cities, regions, or countries.

The Teacher's Role

What is the teacher's role in an active-learning classroom? Is there still a place, for example, for teacher-directed instruction?

Yes, there are appropriate times for teacher-directed instruction, even in an active-learning classroom. Teacher-directed, whole-group instruction may be the most effective choice, for example, when initiating a lesson, building enthusiasm, or checking for understanding. However, to be effective, direct, teacher-led instruction must be balanced by small-group collaboration and individual exploration.

Recently, I had the experience of redesigning a face-to-face professional development presentation as an online class. What a learning experience that was! I had delivered the face-to-face presentation some thirty times, but it still took me more than twenty hours to replicate the content for the online version. The guidelines said that interactivity with the participants in the online class needed to take place every four to five minutes. This challenge subsequently made me rethink my face-to-face teaching. Interactive "breaks" are important to refocus learners, to re-engage them with the content, and to encourage everyone in the class—whether online or face to face—to participate.

This experience brought home a key point about the teacher's role in an active-learning classroom. Learning is social, and it should be fun. The teacher should not be the one doing all the work, which often seems to be the case with the "stand and deliver" mode of teaching. A teacher standing at the front of the classroom and writing on a whiteboard for a prolonged time is not engaging. And passive students are not learning to maximum advantage. Classrooms at all levels need to be structured to focus fully on student engagement of all sorts—with the teacher, with content, and with other students.

Creating an Emotional Connection

Related to engagement is the need for students to be emotionally connected to the process of learning. This concept of connecting students emotionally is important and often overlooked. Students work harder when they are interested, emotionally hooked, and care about what they are studying. Research in neuroscience has yielded some interesting and pertinent findings. For example, researcher Joseph LeDoux (1994) reported that emotions have their own memory pathways and that, as a source of information, emotions are vital to learning. Similarly, "research indicates when emotions are engaged right after a learning experience, the memories are much more likely to be recalled and accuracy goes up" (McGaugh et al., in Jensen, 1998, p. 80). Young people's natural affinity for technology often makes such technology a gateway for emotional, intellectual, and social engagement.

Technology Supports Engagement

Technological tools—hardware and software—can help engage students in amazing ways, but only if the teacher develops and organizes lessons with a clear focus on engagement. Technology supports engagement, not the other way around. Many of the tools discussed in this and later chapters can help students reflect on and interact with content in ways wholly unlike those available in traditional pencil-and-paper classrooms.

Taking what we know about effective instruction for active learning, we can design lessons to incorporate technological tools to increase student participation and interest. The sections that follow illustrate a few sample forms of technology, both hardware and software, that can play a role in engagement that facilitates connections between teacher and students, students and peers, and students and content.

Student Response Systems

In classes or lessons that require substantial direct instruction, teachers can increase student participation by using an electronic student response system. (These devices sometimes are called "clickers.") Here's how it works: The teacher poses a question, and each student responds by pressing a button on an individual, hand-held device. Signals from the students' devices go through a transponder connected to the teacher's computer, and the students' collective responses are immediately displayed in a manner established by the teacher. For example, the responses might be aggregated in a bar graph, showing the number of students responding correctly or incorrectly.

This type of system can provide a highly efficient means of checking for understanding during a lesson, as it allows for immediate formative assessment. Thus, the teacher can rapidly respond to misunderstandings by reteaching or modifying the lesson during the class session.

Another significant advantage is that teachers can see at a glance whether all students are engaged. The disaffected student, who often can elude detection by the teacher in a crowded classroom, cannot hide from the student response system. An optional benefit of such a system is automated recordkeeping, as students' responses can be sent electronically to the teacher's computer-based gradebook.

I brought a student response system home to test with my then twelve-year-old son. His comment has stuck with me: "Mom, no one knows I'm wrong! This is cool!" What a boon to students who are too intimidated to raise their hands and volunteer an answer in class! This feature builds students' confidence and emotional investment in learning. I did not take my son deeper into the software and show him that, in fact, the teacher knows every button a student presses, and there is a record. He did not need to know that, but actually this feature is one of the most powerful aspects of this technology: it collects data for every question from every student. The system thereby provides a powerful way to gather and organize data to paint an accurate portrait of student achievement by lesson, by class, or across several classes.

Student response systems are sold under various brand names, including:

SMART Response by SMART Technologies (formerly Senteo) (www.smarttech.com)

ActiVote by Promethean (www.prometheanworld.com/server .php?show=nav.16)

Qwizdom by Qwizdom Incorporated (www.qwizdom.com)

CPSPulse by eInstruction (www.einstruction.com/products/ assessment/index.html)

TurningPoint Audience Response System by Turning Technologies (www.turningtechnologies.com)

Most systems cost between $1,200 and $1,500 for a classroom set of 30–32 student units.

Student response systems also offer collateral benefits. Some teachers use these systems for collecting other types of information, from who has turned in permission slips or homework to who remembered the word of the day. Most of the systems on the market also have a work-at-your-own-pace feature, which makes it possible for a teacher to hand out, post, or project a test or quiz and then permit students to key their answers into their devices rather than use traditional paper answer sheets. As soon as students submit their responses, the test is graded and recorded in the gradebook, leaving the teacher with more time for other work.

Two concerns come to mind about student response systems. First, these are not systems that can be easily shared. Too often in education, economic necessity forces schools or districts to buy such electronic devices with the idea that teachers will share them. Unfortunately, when systems like these are intended to be shared, the inconvenience of doing so often means that they end up in storage cupboards, not classrooms. Student response systems, to be used effectively, need to be consistently (if not constantly) available to each teacher. And they cannot be forced on teachers. Some teachers are eager adopters of this technology. Those who embrace this technology and become proficient and creative in its use then become the experts who will encourage and support those who were initially reticent.

A second concern is that a student response system should be used in a more meaningful way than as an electronic replacement for worksheets. Clickers are best used to enhance student engagement. For example, they also can be employed to activate schema before a lesson, build curiosity and emotional investment, and start or extend a meaningful class discussion.

Cell Phones

Many schools have banned cell phones, but these ubiquitous and sometimes annoying devices can serve educational purposes. For example, instead of paying for clickers, a cell phone, a text plan, and a website can be used to collect data from students in a way similar to that of a student response system. The teacher sets up a free account on Poll Everywhere (www.polleverywhere.com). He or she then registers questions and launches the poll for students. Each response choice on the poll has a different code that students must text from their cell phones, and students' answers are immediately displayed in a bar graph. While basic plans are free, there also are various pricing plans that allow for more control and the ability to share an account with others. Paid plans start at $15 a month, which permits fifty responses to be received at once and includes other features. Many people are familiar with this type of cell-phone voting from audience-participation shows, such as *American Idol* and *Dancing With the Stars*.

I used Poll Everywhere recently with a middle school staff, and it really was interesting. Like most faculties, this one included a wide range of ages and experience. The younger set had no problems; they entered their answers immediately. Then they turned to help their colleagues. For some of the older set, it was the first text message they had ever sent. There followed a rich discussion about how this technology-mediated strategy could be used with students. The discussion also extended to other potential educational applications of cell phones, such as using some of the tools that are included on most phones, such as calendars for assignments and calculators.

When working with administrators, I often bring up the educational uses of cell phones. Some administrators are skeptical, but I believe that today's advanced cell phones are really miniature personal computers. That makes them potentially powerful learning tools. Of course, schools do not want students merely texting one another or cell phones ringing during class. But banning or locking up this and similar technology during the school day limits learning. I will touch on cell phone use at various points throughout this book, but a few final examples of this tool's educational potential merit inclusion here.

Not long ago, as I was reviewing the school supply list for my eighth-grade son, Patrick, at the beginning of the school year, I was struck by how expensive and wasteful it was to buy a graphing calculator when my son could download a superior calculator application for his iPod touch (discussed in more detail on page 27) for only $1.99. Instead of allowing students like Patrick to use a tool they already own, schools force parents to spend more than a hundred dollars on old technology while the more powerful technology of the iPod touch, the iPhone, or a similar device is confined to students' lockers.

Sending text messages using a cell phone or other texting device such as an iPod touch concerns many educators. Seen in a negative light, texting can pose a distraction or be used for cheating. But the texting feature also has positive educational applications if educators are willing to structure phone-use guidelines accordingly, including specifically incorporating texting into lessons. Most middle school and high school students have mastered the art of texting in their pockets. Why not have the students put their cell phones on their desks—where you can see the screen and any texting activity—and use them in the course of their lessons? Then cell phones can be incorporated into teaching and learning.

A high school coach recently related an experience that he had with one of his players regarding cell phone use. They were on the team bus on the way to a game, and the student was concerned about getting a paper completed on time for class. The coach had observed the boy texting earlier and suggested that he use his phone to begin the writing assignment. The student opened an email, and off he went, thumb-typing away. Later, the student emailed what he had written to himself and completed the final editing on his home computer.

Now if you had asked me to use a cell phone to compose something longer than a text message, I could do it, but it would take me five times as long as it would take using a computer. On the other hand, many (perhaps most) middle school students and older are completely at home using cell phone keyboards, typing solely with two thumbs.

Another feature of most cell phones is a built-in camera, sometimes even a video camera. As long as students are not snapping inappropriate pictures, the camera can be a powerful learning tool. Many classes present opportunities for student-produced media, which can enhance engagement and deepen content understanding. By allowing students to utilize their personal tools, they have ready access to technology that supports "just in time" learning (as opposed to needing to sign up weeks in advance to check out a camera from the media center, for example).

Appropriate use of any technology is crucial, and schools can achieve this goal through dialogue and education, not only with students but also with teachers, parents, and administrators. As cell phone technology becomes commonplace and more versatile, school systems need to review their policies about cell phone use.

Access to technology must not be taken for granted—not every student has a cell phone or an unlimited texting plan—but it need not prevent us from using cell phones at all. Students can be grouped to share cell phones or smartphones with unlimited texting, thus ameliorating the problem and access while facilitating valuable collaboration skills in the process—and students love it!

As educators, we should not be afraid to use the technology that our students already know how to use, and in fact use often and adeptly. But we must establish reasonable expectations for educational uses and build in consequences for misuse.

Skype

Skype (www.skype.com), a free service used daily by millions of individuals and businesses around the globe, is software that marries the functions of the telephone and the computer. Skype software allows users to make free phone calls over the Internet—computer to computer—no matter where those computers are located. While only a microphone is needed to Skype, a webcam provides for a richer experience. The application is free to download and works worldwide. Users also can use Skype to call landlines and cell phones, but there are charges for those kinds of calls. Skype applications also are available for handheld devices, such as the iPod touch and the iPhone.

There are many uses for Skype in the classroom. For example, a foreign language teacher can connect with a class in another country and provide students with experience interacting with native speakers. An expert from a distant zoo can come into a classroom through Skype to talk about animal habitats. A language arts class can make interviewing an author a meaningful part of studying the author's book. Local legislators can join a classroom debate on a topic about which students are writing. Many potential resource persons are willing to Skype (yes, it has become a verb) because doing so saves them from traveling or taking time away from their workplace. All of these activities exemplify active learning through engagement among students, teachers, and outside resource persons.

Although there are many benefits to using Skype, there are a few potential drawbacks. Time zones can be a problem when collaborating with a classroom in another part of the world, and potentially a lesson could be interrupted by someone Skyping into class. However, the interruptions can be controlled by setting the status of your availability.

The Next Big Tool for Active Learning

Earlier I mentioned the iPod touch in passing. This versatile mini-computer represents a transformation in the making, certainly supplementing if not supplanting in some cases the standard-size computer or laptop. Its features make it an excellent tool for active learning.

Apple's iPod touch has everything the company's popular iPhone has, except the phone and the expense of an accompanying data plan. These sleek, compact computers can do almost everything a full-size computer can do, although there are obvious limitations because of their small size. For example, it's difficult to write at length on an iPod touch, and certain applications limit interactivity more than their full-scale versions do.

The iPod touch connects to the Internet through a wireless connection, and then applications can be downloaded free or for a small fee (such as $1.99 for the graphing calculator app). These applications provide all sorts of programs that can facilitate active learning, including instructional games, simulations, readers, flashcards, and so forth. You name it, and there's an app for it. My friend Scott Meech (www.smeech.net), a district technology facilitator in Kenilworth, Illinois, is doing some interesting research about these devices in education. You can follow his journey and learn about his suggested apps for education on his website, I Education Apps Review (www.iear.org), which focuses mainly on Apple "i" products, such as the iPhone, iPod, and related technology.

The iPod touch has a big brother, the Apple iPad. Like the iPod touch, the Apple iPad runs applications and connects to the Internet wirelessly. Google has announced a partnership with Verizon to produce an interactive pad that will compete with Apple's iPad. There is already a movement by textbook publishers to move their books to the iPad, and I am sure the same thing will happen with the other pads that will be released.

Clearly, the huge variety of downloadable apps for the iPod touch is a major selling point. But its capabilities also make this device a powerful technological tool that should be embraced by schools. Similar to the case that I and others make for allowing cell phones in schools, I would argue that education policymakers need to consider new rules and allow—even encourage—teachers and students to use the iPod touch and related technological tools to activate learning in new, exciting, relevant ways.

For the cost-conscious, it is possible to economize in some ways with the iPod touch. For example, an inexpensive hub (priced around $10) will allow one iPod touch to power five sets of earbuds. (One such hub is called RockStar, manufactured by Belkin.) A hub of this type can be used to create a listening center in the classroom.

Many schools are starting to explore how teachers can use the power of the iPod touch in the classroom. Various apps can be used by teachers and students to:

Listen to audiobooks

Review skills (for example, with a flashcard-generator app)

Learn vocabulary

Increase productivity

Collaborate with other students

Get organized (for example, with a calendar app)

Generate lists before or after brainstorming

Solve math problems (for example, with a calculator app)

Create a number line

Take notes

Technology Supports Collaboration

The goal of engagement for active learning also is supported by extensive use of collaboration strategies. Collaboration often goes hand in hand with differentiation of instruction. Tomlinson (2001) notes,

> While it is true that differentiated instruction offers several avenues to learning, it does not assume a separate level for each learner. It also focuses on meaningful learning or powerful ideas for all students. Differentiation is probably more reminiscent of the one-room-schoolhouse than of individualization. That model of instruction recognized that the teacher needed to work sometimes with the whole

> class, sometimes with small groups, and sometimes
> with individuals. These variations were important in
> order both to move each student along in his par-
> ticular understandings and skills as well as to build a
> sense of community in the group. (p. 2)

By allowing students to choose, within defined parameters, what and how to study, teachers encourage students to study in ways that most effectively engage them with content. Collaboration engages students with one another in the pursuit of content knowledge and understanding. While differentiated instruction needs to be carefully planned and monitored, once students are aware of many of the Web 2.0 tools at their command, they will be able to choose those best suited to their needs. Allowing such flexibility often results in a louder classroom but one in which deeper learning takes place.

Web 2.0 tools can facilitate collaboration, which means, for example, that teachers need to explore ways that social networking can be adapted for teaching and learning. Many people not currently involved in social networking on the Internet are apprehensive about it because of news stories that have focused on dangers and abuses, such as cyberbullying. (Cyberbullying is the use of communication technology for deliberate, repeated, hostile behavior.) Appropriately used, however, social networking sites can be stimuli for collaboration—and not only for students.

Two of the best-known social networking sites are MySpace (www .myspace.com) and Facebook (www.facebook.com). The former initially was launched as a way to help garage bands get their music out to fans. (I would not recommend allowing students to have access to MySpace at school. Besides posing a distraction, MySpace has content that is inappropriate and advertising that is even worse.) According to Erick Schonfeld (2009) of TechCrunch, Facebook is the fourth most popular website on the Internet, trailing only Google, Microsoft, and Yahoo!

Following, in no special order, are several other sites (some with downloadable software) that may be helpful for student collaboration in support of active learning. Visit **go.solution-tree.com/ technology** for links to the websites in this book.

LibraryThing

LibraryThing (www.librarything.com) is a social network all about books. It allows users to create their own virtual bookshelves by displaying books they are currently reading or have on their actual bookshelves. After creating a free account, a student can enter the title of a book, which triggers a connection to the Amazon.com database and imports an image of the cover and information about that book.

Once students establish a virtual bookshelf, they can use LibraryThing to find out what other people, including classmates, are reading; read reviews; and join chat-like book discussions. This website can also be used by school librarians and classroom teachers to promote various books, including those that expand or enhance the content of a given lesson. LibraryThing can be accessed by students at school or at home, and so learning can be extended and might even involve other family members. And what a great way to showcase summer reading titles!

A similar network is Shelfari (www.shelfari.com). Shelfari, which is owned by Amazon, offers many features similar to those of LibraryThing, including the ability to build a virtual bookshelf, to see what one's friends are reading, to read and write book reviews, and to participate in book discussions. The site's goal is to bring readers together by facilitating and encouraging substantive discussions.

Ning

Ning (www.ning.com) is an easy-to-use website that welcomes groups, such as classes of students, and provides a social networking platform with just a simple login and password. This is an advertising-supported site, but educators can request that the ads be removed. A network can be left public or locked for privacy, with all controls set by the person establishing the network.

Before I had much experience using a social network, I joined Classroom 2.0 (www.classroom20.com), which was created on the Ning platform. Similar to what can be done with student networks, this one provides for collaborative learning at the professional level. Current Classroom 2.0 membership is about 37,000 educators, all passionate about technology, education, and change. At various times, I have been engaged in inspiring conversations about the current realities of schools and classrooms and ideas that hold promise for the future. Many conversations include threaded discussions, and subgroups have been created to cater to specific interests.

For years Ning was a free solution for groups to create a social network. In July 2010, a new pricing structure was put in place ranging from $20 a year for 150 members to $500 a year for unlimited members.

The power of the network is truly amazing when it comes to making connections and finding like-minded educators. Instead of being limited to the collective knowledge of their school colleagues, teachers can tap into the knowledge and interests of thousands of colleagues worldwide.

A few years ago, I used a Ning network to manage communications and information exchanged with and by students in a graduate class that I was teaching. Throughout the class, all communications and assignments were exchanged through the Ning interface. It was a completely paperless class. I loved teaching in this environment.

School Town

School Town (http://schooltown.net) is an online learning community designed to leverage an instructor's time with organizational and workflow tools. The School Town team is very open to educators' suggestions and responsive to their needs. When I needed a way for my students to post videos and share them with the rest of the class, the team was able to put a solution up quickly and effectively.

The best part of School Town, however, is that it allows for a paperless classroom. Every assignment, chat, and forum discussion is processed digitally through School Town. The teacher has a digital record of every assignment each student has submitted and every interaction that has taken place online. This helps to streamline grading, encourage communication between students, and archive multimedia. The ease of management is the key, and School Town was built to be intuitive and fun.

This low-cost subscription solution has enhanced security features. A parent portal strengthens the home-school connection and keeps parents in the loop regarding assignments and performance. School Town allows a classroom to collaborate beyond the bricks and mortar, making it possible to chat, discuss, and share resources long after the school day is over.

Delicious

Collaboration often involves students sharing resources that they have found on the Internet with their classmates. One popular and easy-to-use tool is a bookmarking site called Delicious (http://delicious.com). Once teachers or students create a free account, they can log in and bookmark Internet resources they have found. Users also can organize their resources and tag keywords. The site is always available, and so students can work at home as well as in school. This is a convenient service, and the collaborative element of students sharing their bookmarks with others is powerful. This form of collaboration can make major learning projects easier because several students can share responsibility for the research task.

Google Docs

One of the most powerful Web 2.0 tools for collaboration is Google Docs (http://docs.google.com). This free website can help small and large groups work interactively and share documents. Each document that a user or group creates can be shared with others, making it possible to work with a variety of groups, depending on the project. Google Docs currently provides for word processing (to create documents such as letters and reports) and other template-based applications, such as presentations, spreadsheets, folders, drawings, and forms. Dictionary and translation programs are built in.

Google Docs can help teachers and students stay organized, for example, by placing documents in folders. Files are continuously backed up so that data won't be lost, and documents are stored on a Google server, making it possible to access them anyplace with an Internet connection. A newer feature of Google Docs permits users to work with documents offline and then sync them with the online version after reconnecting.

All of these features are exciting, but the real power of Google Docs lies in the potential for collaborative learning. The website allows up to two hundred collaborators to work on a document virtually simultaneously. Consider peer editing. After students share a new document, a notification window shows the writer the names of others who are currently editing it, and color-coding helps students more easily see who is working on the document. When all of the peer editors have weighed in, the writer can change the type color back to black and file or print the final document.

One weakness of the Google Docs application is the limited number of built-in features; however, there is an easy fix. If more extensive editing is needed, students can easily export their document to Microsoft Word or some other text program. One big advantage of Google Docs is that the website takes away any formatting compatibility issues between Macs and PCs or between various versions of word-processing software.

Teachers will appreciate the revision-history feature, which details every contribution to a given document. The revision-history logs facilitate recordkeeping (for example, who participated in peer editing and to what extent) and grading. And if a peer reviewer inadvertently deletes something, the writer can revert to an earlier revision to restore lost text—no more student complaints about lost papers.

Creative collaborative uses of Google Docs in schools include facilitating grade-level communication logs and committee and administrative communications. The website also can be used by articulation teams, school-improvement planning groups, and buildingwide collaboration teams.

Google Apps Education Edition

Google Apps Education Edition(www.google.com/a/help/intl/en/edu/index.html), which includes Google Docs, is a broader, school-oriented Google website especially created for education. There are numerous benefits with Google Apps Education Edition, from backing up data to 24/7 access without compromising the school network.

There are many additional features in Google Apps Education Edition, which I will touch on at various points in this book. For example, the site allows students to obtain school-approved email addresses (through Google's Gmail service). However, this feature can be turned off if school officials do not want to provide students with email access.

Google Apps Education Edition is free—and ad-free. Moreover, the Web 2.0 tools are transportable, meaning that the same or similar apps can be used on standard desktop and laptop computers as well as mini-computers, ranging from smartphones (iPhone, BlackBerry, Droid) to the iPod touch and slightly larger (but still small) computers, such as netbooks (also called mini-notebooks or ultraportables).

Google SketchUp

Google SketchUp (http://sketchup.google.com/download) is free design software for creating three-dimensional models. This 3-D modeling software is amazingly powerful, even in comparison to its pro version (which is not free) or more sophisticated design programs, such as CAD (computer-aided design) software. Students as young as preschoolers conceivably could use the Google SketchUp software.

Students can get started in Google SketchUp by creating a basic shape and then using a push/pull feature to expand it into a 3-D shape. Shapes can be pushed to various heights, and then the sides of the shapes can be "painted" using various built-in textures and colors. More advanced features include such things as a measuring tool to build to scale, a labeling feature, a moviemaking feature, and more. There also is a 3-D warehouse from which various component objects can be downloaded and rescaled for a student's individual or group project. Objects include seemingly everything, from a backyard swing set to an aircraft carrier. There also are collections, such as objects related to alternative energy, history in general, castles, and so on.

A group of upper elementary teachers wanted to incorporate Google SketchUp into the curriculum. In the past, they had assigned a project that required students to build a physical model of an animal cell. The teachers decided this time to work with students to create 3-D models of the cell in Google SketchUp and were thrilled by how excited their young students were to tackle the project. Many of the students liked Google SketchUp so much that they went home, downloaded the software to their personal computers, and created their own dream homes. A number of the teachers now use Google SketchUp as a station in their classrooms to extend learning whenever students have completed other work.

One word of caution is worth mentioning: the design files in this program become extremely large when students add a number of elements from the 3-D warehouse, and so digital storage capacity can be an issue.

In addition to visiting the Google SketchUp website, those of you who want to know more can check out some eight thousand videos about Google SketchUp that have been uploaded on YouTube (www.youtube.com). An excellent example among these contributions is one about autistic students working with the design software (www.youtube.com/watch?v=k7PIwSnKq7E).

Some Google SketchUp project ideas include designing:

A stage set for the school play

Models of new learning spaces

Various buildings in the community

A floor plan for a room—bedroom, classroom, and so on

A historically accurate or fictional castle

An animal habitat

Building Digital-Rich Curricula

If students are not engaged with content lesson by lesson, then, as educators, we've lost them. In both high-performing and struggling schools, teachers, administrators, and policymakers need to address the need for increasing student engagement by building a digital-rich curriculum. Such a curriculum is needed to mirror technology use beyond the schoolhouse door, where young people and adults alike are daily immersed in a digital world. Even high-performing schools need to examine curriculum and instruction to ensure that students are actively learning and collaborating to amplify the acquisition of new knowledge and skills. High test scores do not equal high engagement. In many of our so-called best classrooms, students are bored to death!

The hardware and software sampled in this chapter are illustrative of technology that can increase engagement and collaboration. These are tools—most with some inclusion of Web 2.0—that all of us see in use, in some form, every day. Business authors Don Tapscott and Anthony D. Williams (2006) make the point this way:

> Billions of connected individuals can now actively participate in innovation, wealth creation, and social development in ways we once only dreamed of. And when these masses of people collaborate they collectively can advance the arts, culture, science, education, government, and the economy in surprising but ultimately profitable ways. Companies that engage with these exploding Web-enabled communities are already discovering the true dividends of collective capability and genius. (p. 3)

In schools with digital-rich curricula and classroom environments enlivened by engagement and collaboration for active learning, the "true dividends" are high achievement by students who are motivated and involved and eagerly want to learn.

chapter 3

Technology to Support Teaching and Learning

Earlier, I stated that merely outfitting schools with technology does not automatically transform passive classrooms into ones of high engagement. Lessons need to be defined or redefined, and substantive changes are crucial. This means that teachers (and administrators) must look beyond the bells and whistles of available technology. Yes, many forms of technology are captivating and fun to use, but the real role of technology in classrooms is not to entertain but to facilitate learning in new, active, engaging, and collaborative ways.

If students are to become critical thinkers, then we must assign projects that stimulate their engagement, not just worksheets. An active-learning orientation would suggest that they need to be engaged in meaningful projects—analyzing and synthesizing content, not merely absorbing it from readings or discussions. For example, when students produce a video that takes a historic speech and matches it with complementary images, accomplishing this project promotes deeper understanding as they study the speech to discern which images will best convey the speaker's ideas.

Bloom's taxonomy is a seminal work in the field of education because it redefined meaningful learning. Although it was created in the 1950s, it is still relevant because it can help teachers design lessons that incorporate higher-order thinking skills. Educational technology expert Andrew Churches (2009) adapted Bloom's taxonomy to bring it into the 21st century, employing tools that Bloom could not have imagined (see fig. 3.1, page 40). The goal of

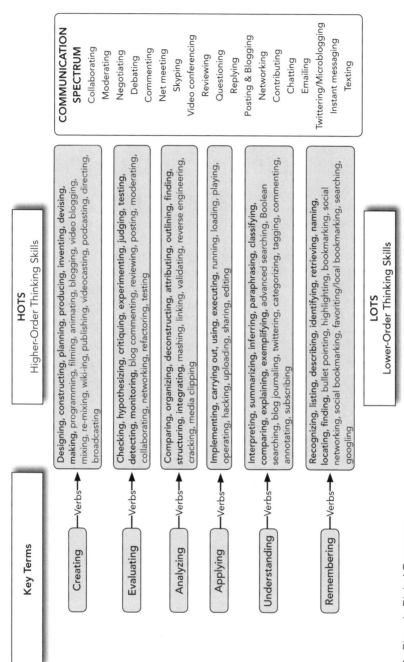

Figure 3.1: Bloom's Digital Taxonomy.

Source: Adapted from Churches, 2009. Used with permission.

education is to move students to the top, away from simply remembering isolated facts toward fully integrated thinking at the highest levels. Because students will be starting at various levels, instruction needs to be differentiated using tiered activities to meet the needs of all learners. Integrating technology in these activities can create new learning possibilities that can improve teachers' ability to reach all students, usually within the context of the same project.

Students crave engagement, and technology is the language they speak. Opening with a video clip or a sound bite can initiate a lesson in an engaging way and thus draw in students who might otherwise be uninterested. Having students actually create media moves a lesson upward in Bloom's taxonomy and exemplifies the transition from passive learning to active engagement.

Imagine, for example, asking students to select a historic speech to serve as the centerpiece or storyline of a media presentation that they will create. Small groups of students will research the themes of the speech, find out about the historical era, and identify the significance of the speech. For instance, students might be directed to the website of the National Archives (www.archives. gov), where they can find an audio clip from President Franklin D. Roosevelt's December 8, 1941, "Day of Infamy" speech, which preceded by only days America's declaration of war on Japan during World War II. Teachers will find that the National Archives website holds many instructional resources, including lesson plans, audio and video clips, facsimile documents, and links to additional resources. But the Internet is rich in similar kinds of sites for all subject areas.

In this lesson, students will create new media by combining what they find on the National Archives website and other sites with traditional library research, readings from their textbooks, and original writing. The resulting media presentations might take a number of forms by combining images (still and video), spoken word, music, and so forth. The result might be an audio recording, a video made using easily accessible moviemaking software, or a sound-and-image presentation.

Standards-Aligned Classrooms

National, state or provincial, and local standards have been created for most, if not all, areas of the school curriculum. These standards define what students should know and be able to do. Standards should be a driving force when planning what to teach in a given subject. Often the textbook becomes the driving force, but like technology, textbooks are instructional tools.

To keep standards at the forefront of planning, teaching, and learning, the standards should be clearly translated into specific lesson objectives, and these objectives should be posted and discussed with students. This helps keep teachers and students on the same course toward achieving the objectives. From observing and coaching in a variety of schools, I have found that teachers who post objectives tend to plan and conduct lessons that are better aligned to adopted standards than teachers who don't.

There are also standards for technology. The International Society for Technology in Education (ISTE) has defined National Educational Technology Standards (NETS) for students, teachers, and administrators. These detailed standards are being adopted by many states as expected benchmarks. The standards for each group can be accessed and read in full or downloaded as PDFs (www.iste .org/AM/Template.cfm?Section=NETS).

As of the writing of this book, the student NETS categories—which include performance indicators—are as follows:

- ☐ Creativity and innovation
- ☐ Communication and collaboration
- ☐ Research and information fluency
- ☐ Critical thinking, problem solving, and decision making
- ☐ Digital citizenship
- ☐ Technology operations and concepts

Integrating Standards and Technology

With the goal of keeping standards foremost, how can teachers integrate technology and instruction? In figure 3.1 (page 40), the graphic created by Andrew Churches marries Bloom's taxonomy with technology-mediated strategies—for example, podcasting, blogging, and animating—to create what Churches calls Bloom's Digital Taxonomy. This taxonomy illustrates how the use of Web 2.0 and related tools can help teachers design engaging, standards-linked lessons. At the top of Churches' redesigned taxonomy is "creating," which replaces Bloom's original "evaluation."

Wikis

Among the technology-mediated strategies for creative collaboration, Churches includes using wikis. The term *wiki* means "fast" in Hawaiian, and the association is apt. This is particularly true with regard to the largest wiki: Wikipedia (www.wikipedia.org). A wiki allows multiple users to compose, edit, and view documents, making it possible for a large number of people to be, literally, on the same page. Wikipedia exemplifies this functionality. This popular online encyclopedia is written, edited, and critiqued—as well as consulted—by users worldwide. Because anyone can contribute to Wikipedia, students need to use this as a secondary instead of primary resource for information.

A well-designed wiki is a timesaver when working with student groups of all sizes. Wiki documents, for example, don't need to be printed or emailed back and forth. Instead, all documents related to a project can be kept in one online location to be accessed by individual students and groups at any time.

Many teachers organize their digital classrooms with a wiki. The wiki makes it possible to teach paperlessly by exchanging files through the wiki. A teacher can also use the discussion feature to focus students on a topic. Some teachers join their students on the wiki the evening before a test to help answer any last-minute questions. Homework can be posted to the wiki along with frequently needed forms.

Preparing students for the future workplace should be the goal of every educator. With this in mind, educators may find Don Tapscott and Anthony D. Williams' *Wikinomics: How Mass Collaboration Changes Everything* to be of particular interest. The book discusses why businesses need to shift practices from controlling the flow of information to a collaborative, wiki-style culture of collaboration—and how such a shift can be accomplished. Throughout the book, originally published in 2006, the authors illustrate, in essence, how NETS work in the real world. They include numerous stories about how businesses, including large corporations, are embracing social media in a variety of ways to make their goods or services better and to gain a competitive edge.

Google Earth

Google increasingly is becoming a generic term. "To google" is now standard shorthand meaning "to search the Internet." Google is, in fact, a large toolbox of Web 2.0 tools that can be used to implement standards-driven instruction. In chapter 2, I touched on three of these tools: Google Docs, Google Apps Education Edition, and Google SketchUp. Let's now look at a fourth: Google Earth.

Any curricular area can be designed (or redesigned) to be relevant and to help students develop lifelong learning skills. Google Earth provides an excellent tool to accomplish these ends. For example, a colleague used it for a seventh-grade history assignment about explorers. Students were tasked to identify fifteen points of interest that Lewis and Clark would find along their route to the Pacific Ocean if they returned today and repeated their trek. The teacher's objectives, based on the standards for this subject, were (1) to reinforce students' knowledge of the route taken by the Lewis and Clark expedition, (2) to expand students' knowledge of geography, and (3) to teach basic Internet research skills (also a NETS performance indicator). Previously, when the teacher taught this lesson, the students illustrated their points of interest by sketching the sites on sticky notes that they then affixed to a wall map.

The students had enjoyed the assignment in the past, but not everyone was an artist. So the teacher wanted to do something new. Together, she and I restructured the lesson using free software for

Google Earth (http://earth.google.com). Google Earth allows users to combine various media in innovative ways. One of the features, for instance, allows users to insert virtual pushpins into a computerized map. Students can key in (or copy and paste) their research about each point of interest on the pushpin at that location. When students finish with all of their pushpins, they can save the file and then share their virtual tour with others through email or by posting to a blog, a wiki, or a website.

I suggested that the students work in groups because Google Earth can strain network capacity (known as bandwidth). Following the lesson, the teacher reported that her students loved the project and were thinking of other ways to use Google Earth.

When the teacher and I were preparing this lesson, a comment by cognitive scientist Daniel Willingham (2009) came to mind: "If memory is the residue of thought, the students will remember incorrect 'discoveries' as much as they will remember the correct ones" (p. 63). This could not have been truer for us, for as we experimented and explored, we learned as much from our mistakes as we did from our successes. We knew what we wanted to do but had no idea how to do it, so online we went—to Google, to discover and create. We did not attend a class; we had to figure it out ourselves. This is what teaching is today—constantly relearning, reteaching, redesigning, and rethinking.

Technology Supports Differentiated Instruction

While standards are the same for all students, the paths to reach those standards often are as individual as the students themselves. Differentiating the activities that we ask students to do is critical. Instead of having all students in a class doing the same thing, we can structure assignments so that students work on various tasks, using a variety of technological tools as well as print resources. The previous project involving the Lewis and Clark expedition is a case in point. I suggested that the teacher assign students to small groups and give each group a different portion of the expedition route. Then each group could decide how to represent their part of the journey.

Differentiated instruction for the Lewis and Clark project means that student groups can choose from a variety of Web 2.0 and other tools. Example approaches include the following, some of which use tools discussed in later chapters:

Creating a podcast about points of interest

Making a video of each point along the route

Creating a Glog using Glogster

Using Google Earth to create a map with virtual pushpins, images, or embedded videos

Skyping with classes in schools along the route to compare and contrast locations

Creating a mural with images gleaned from the Internet

Using Flickr to gather images and make a collage

Creating a VoiceThread

Using images from the Library of Congress online collection

Using photo-editing software to "photoshop" Lewis and Clark into modern images

Using a blue-screen/green-screen technique so that students can put themselves in a video about the route

Blogging about the journey from the point of view of Lewis or Clark and inviting classmates to comment

Creating a wiki about the group's assigned portion of the journey

Creating a Wordle about the points of interest with hyperlinks

Using ImageChef to generate hints about the selected points of interest

Using Google Docs for group communication

Using Google SketchUp to create 3-D replicas of places Lewis and Clark might have seen

Twittering questions about points of interest

Searching online newspapers to find points of interest to include

Using an online travel site to price a group trip through the assigned region

Technology Facilitates Storytelling

Storytelling is a critical part of our culture. "The human mind seems exquisitely tuned to understand and remember stories," suggests Willingham (2009), "so much so that psychologists sometimes refer to stories as 'psychologically privileged,' meaning that they are treated differently in memory than other types of material. I'm going to suggest that organizing a lesson plan like a story is an effective way to help students comprehend and remember" (pp. 51–52).

Willingham (2009) continues: "First, stories are easy to comprehend, because the audience knows the structure, which helps to interpret the action. . . . Second, stories are interesting. . . . Third, stories are easy to remember" (pp. 52–53).

Danny's Story

Changing how students construct stories or reports about something they have read from the standard pen-and-paper approach to multimedia can help all young readers. In fact, some of the technological tools students can use actually will help students think in new ways about text. Let's examine one student's digital book report project. For this example, I am using my son Danny.

At the time, Danny was a fifth-grade student who dreaded reading. He was reading below grade level, and book reports were one of the tasks with which he struggled most. The librarian helped him locate a high-interest/low-vocabulary book, which he brought home to share with me. We would alternate shared reading: I would read a page aloud, and then he would struggle to read a page. To our delight, we found that this book was set close to where we were living.

Danny was fascinated by weather, and this book was about a tornado that hit a nearby suburb a few years before Danny was born. I remembered the day of the tornado vividly and was able to share my stories with him. These stories helped Danny activate his schema to better relate to the text. Daniel Pink (2005) tells us,

> Story represents a pathway to understanding that
> doesn't run through the left side of the brain. We

> can see this yearning for self-knowledge through
> stories in many places—in the astonishingly popu-
> lar "scrapbooking" movement, where people assem-
> ble the artifacts of their lives into a narrative that
> tells the world, and maybe themselves, who they are
> and what they're about, and in the surging popular-
> ity of genealogy as millions search the Web to piece
> together their family histories. (p. 115)

I believe this was one of the first books Danny *enjoyed* reading. But then there was the book report to do—and how would that go?

Fortunately, Danny's teacher allowed her students to pick projects that interested them. Danny wanted to make a documentary movie because he was interested in telling his story, not writing it. Writing, like reading, was very difficult for him.

I introduced him to the technological tools he could use to make his digital story. (I discuss these and related tools later in this chapter.) I wasn't going to do Danny's work for him, and I remember actually sitting on my hands as we sat together working. As his guide, I taught him how to search Google for images to incorporate in his report. After collecting images and saving them to a folder, Danny started putting them in the order he wanted to tell the story. He arranged some fifteen images, and then he was ready to record the narration.

We plugged in a microphone, and Danny started to tell his story. We soon found that this part of the project was quite challenging, more so than we had expected. The narration for the first image slide consumed nine "takes" before Danny finally said what he wanted to say and was satisfied with the result.

In the end, Danny saved his documentary on a flash drive and went off to school, excited about sharing his project. I was happy to know that my son had acquired a new set of skills that would serve him well in future work.

Danny went from dreading a project to being excited about showing his work. There are a couple of important points to make before we get into the how-to. First, by restructuring this project,

Danny was engaged in the creation of the digital story; the technology helped him accomplish his goal. More important, Danny was proud of his work. The project focused on his verbal strengths instead of his weaknesses in spelling and writing.

Danny's story goes beyond merely creating a presentation and receiving a grade. This realization came when Danny and I sat down for the next book report with another book in the series. After I read a page, he read a page, and then he stopped me and said, "Mom! Wait! I see pictures in my head! This time, can we start the presentation with a clip of thunder and lightning and get everyone's attention, and then tell the story?" I remember it like it was yesterday.

Good readers make pictures in their heads and storyboard the action *as* they read. Struggling readers are so busy trying to figure out the words and what they mean that they don't make mental pictures. Patricia Wolfe (2001), a noted researcher in brain-based learning, explains, "Working memory is indeed limited. Still, before we become too discouraged with its space limitations, we need to realize that these limitations can be circumvented somewhat by the ability to 'chunk' information. . . . A chunk is defined as any meaningful unit of information" (p. 10). Collecting images and storyboarding the first book report using the moviemaking strategy had given Danny a lifelong skill that many fluent readers take for granted.

Resources for Digital Storytelling

Keep in mind that this concept of the story as a lesson organizer should be at the instructional forefront, not the media or the applications to manipulate them. Too often, the opposite occurs—even in professional development activities. We end up focusing on the technology rather than what we aim to accomplish instructionally *through* technology. Even if the technology consists of only a collection of images and an audio recording, it is the guiding attention to story that must direct how students and teachers select and use technology. Some examples of useful technology follow.

Responsible Digital Citizenship

Multimedia projects, like the one Danny created, combine media from a variety of sources, resulting in the delivery of a new, unique message or product. Creating this new product, called a mashup, requires teachers and students to consider some basic legal and ethical issues concerning who owns the media elements being mashed up. In the National Educational Technology Standards for Students (NETS-S), Standard 5 states: "Students understand human, cultural, and societal issues related to technology and practice legal and ethical behavior."

Therefore, I caution teachers who work with students to gather still images, video clips, and so on to be mindful of legal ownership, which usually refers to copyright. Many online resources provide in-depth copyright information, for example, K–12 Copyright Laws: Primer for Teachers (www.edu-cyberpg. com/Teachers/copyrightlaw.html). However, one of the easiest ways to model ethical behavior (and avoid running afoul of copyright restrictions) is to search for media that are licensed under Creative Commons (http://creativecommons.org).

According to its website description, Creative Commons "is a nonprofit organization that increases sharing and improves collaboration." Basically, Creative Commons gives permission to use a selected image, video clip, or audio clip, but requests that users not resell the media. Users can mash up the media and remix them for personal—including educational—use.

In the ever-changing Web 2.0 world, students need to learn what can and cannot be used for digital projects. Understanding limits, such as copyright, should be part of the curriculum. Many people believe that whatever they find on YouTube is copyright free, and therefore free to use. This is not the case. However, if media are licensed under Creative Commons, that fact usually is clearly displayed. As a rule of thumb, teachers should require students to copy the source web address (URL) of each piece of media along with the media images or clips themselves whenever they assemble a mashup.

Working With Still Images: Photo Story, Flickr, iPhoto, and iTunes

Powerful still images can help students make pictures in their heads, or chunk information, as previously discussed. Working with still images is easier than working with video clips, making still images a good way to get started.

Because many images found on the Internet are copyrighted, it is helpful to have a go-to photo resource. One of these is Flickr (www.flickr.com), one of the largest databases for images and videos. Many of the uploaded images are copyrighted, but you can search using the "advanced" feature and select the Creative Commons licensing option, which will weed out most of the copyrighted images.

Mac computers come with iPhoto preinstalled. This software allows users to organize, crop, retouch, and otherwise manipulate photographic images. The iPhoto program is designed to integrate with iTunes, the Mac-based music software that allows users to create their own digital music collection, and iDVD. Apple software tends to be intuitive and thus easy to learn, though some elements are more challenging than others.

PC users can download free Microsoft Photo Story 3 (www.microsoft .com/windowsxp/using/digitalphotography/photostory/default. mspx). Photo Story has a built-in fade-in/fade-out transition capability and an easy-to-use interface to add copyright-free music, which can be generated within the program. Using Photo Story, students can add music from a CD or personally narrate the presentation, as Danny did for his tornado story project. Photo Story software is easy to download, install, and use.

Image transitions also can be set by selecting parts of the image and using a zoom-in/zoom-out feature. For example, you may want to start a slide by focusing on one student in a group and then have the slide zoom out to include the whole group. The transitions can be adjusted for a set amount of time. However, neither iPhoto nor Photo Story was designed to time the images to a soundtrack; they are designed simply to let the music play behind the images. If the goal is to time images to words and music, then the user will need to step up to more sophisticated video-editing software. Untimed background narration by students is a satisfactory option in most cases. And, for that, the only requirement is a quiet room and a microphone.

Working With Moving Images: Movie Maker, Adobe Premiere Elements, iMovie, and iDVD

If you recall, Danny started his book report by searching for pictures. He found several licensed under Creative Commons and saved them in a desktop folder. Next, he used the free PC-based Windows Movie Maker program (often found in the Accessories folder) to begin constructing his presentation.

In my experience, this moviemaking software tends to lock up, or freeze, so saving work often is important. But it is part of the Windows bundle of software and free of charge, so I've continued to use it in spite of this drawback.

For larger projects on a PC, I have purchased Adobe Premiere Elements, which is one of the many readily available video-editing software packages that will take users to a higher level of technological sophistication. It is more stable than Movie Maker and allows the user to burn DVDs with menus and themes that look professional.

Mac computer users can access iMovie, which is far more stable and easier to use than Movie Maker. The iMovie program seamlessly integrates with iDVD, the Mac-based software to make and burn DVDs, to create truly professional-quality productions. Mac users may have a steeper learning curve to use the more sophisticated features of iMovie, but the coordination with iDVD removes many of the challenges found on the PC side.

Working With Sound: Freeplay Music, Library of Congress, and Royalty Free Music.com

Students can use a microphone to narrate their work, and this is a great way to develop their fluency. Commercially produced music or spoken-word CDs—including collections gathered and downloaded from iTunes—fall under copyright protection. Short samples may be used without infringing on copyright, but restrictions

Numerous sites have images that are not appropriate for all students. Following are a few possible teacher tools; however, they should be previewed before allowing students to use them. Visit **go.solution-tree.com/technology** for links to the websites in this book.

Add Letters generates your name on various signs: www.addletters.com

BeFunky allows you to apply effects to digital photos: www.befunky.com

Big Huge Labs offers several tools to manipulate photos: http://bighugelabs.com

FACEinHOLE.com allows you to select a new body on which to place your face: www.faceinhole.com

Fun Photo Box offers several effects to create funny photos: http://funphotobox.com

ImageChef generates an image from available templates: www.imagechef.com

JibJab allows you to create your own JibJab: http://sendables.jibjab.com

Loonapix allows you to put your face on various templates: www.loonapix.com

MagMyPic allows you to create fun magazine covers: www.magmypic.com

MushyGushy allows you to put your face into various animated scenes: www.mushygushy.com

myFrame.us allows you to frame your pictures for free: http://myframe.us

My Movie Moment allows you to add an image to a movie clip: http://mymoviemoment.com

Photo505 offers effects to manipulate photos: www.photo505.com

PhotoFunia allows you to put your face on Mount Rushmore and more: http://photofunia.com

PicArtia allows you to create photo mosaics: www.makeuseof .com/dir/picartia

Pimp the Face allows you to change or create a face: www.pimptheface.com

Space Your Face allows you to put your face on a dancing astronaut: http://spaceyourface.nasa.gov

may be quite limiting. A number of websites provide copyright-free audio; however, they should be used with caution. Sometimes individuals place music on their websites without knowing or indicating that the music is copyrighted. Reliable Internet sources include the commercial site Freeplay Music (http://freeplaymusic.com) and the Library of Congress (www.loc.gov/index.html), which is a government website. Royalty Free Music.com (www.royaltyfreemusic.com/free-music-resources.html) is another great website; here, artists have uploaded music that can be previewed and downloaded.

Publishing Students' Work

Publishing students' multimedia products provides both validation for the student and a means of assessment for the teacher. In a Web 2.0 world, sharing—showing, posting, publishing—is an extension of digital collaboration. Think of it as going beyond the bulletin board. Putting students' projects on display on the Internet offers a different experience from tacking a project on the classroom bulletin board. Publishing online can invite critical reviews from a wider audience, young and old, beyond the students' peer group.

A number of online formats allow students to share their work with others, such as a personal blog or podcast. A blog (short for "weblog") is an online log that is controlled by its creator; others can post comments, but the creator has the power to filter those comments. A podcast is just a fancy name for an audio file. Anyone can create a podcast about any topic; a computer and a microphone are the only tools needed. School and district websites also are a growing possibility. However, before sharing any student project with the world, make sure this aligns with the district's acceptable use policy, often seen as AUP.

Let's take a look at three of the most popular video-sharing sites. The videos on these three websites are free to upload and to view.

YouTube

YouTube (www.youtube.com) is the largest but also the most controversial site. YouTube will always be controversial because there is not a librarian checking in the videos, organizing them, and checking for appropriate content. Everyone knows that there are innumerable videos on YouTube that are inappropriate for children, but with careful screening, YouTube also offers valuable educational content that is available for free. Often it is blocked in schools, and so teachers may need to explore another option. On any site, teachers need to use caution when posting students' projects. Some, like YouTube, do little to monitor uploads, and some accessible material may be inappropriate for some students.

TeacherTube

TeacherTube.com (http://teachertube.com), launched in 2007, is an education-friendly video site. While this website tends to upload slowly in comparison to the larger YouTube website, it is specifically designed to allow teachers to share lessons and projects. The site has a "channels" feature that assists in searching for relevant materials.

SchoolTube.com

SchoolTube.com (www.schooltube.com), launched in 2006, is a video-sharing website, specifically for K–12 educators and students. It claims to be the largest site with these particular characteristics, and it is endorsed by several national education associations, including both the National Association of Elementary School Principals (NAESP) and National Association of Secondary School Principals (NASSP).

Technology Supports Writing Instruction

Integrating Web 2.0 technology in curriculum and instruction does not mean doing away with basic writing skills, though it may mean thinking beyond the traditional pen and paper. After all, the focus was never the technology of the pen or the paper; it was the writing. And writing remains the focus when newer technologies are employed. Following are a couple of writing-oriented examples of supportive Web 2.0 technology that can help students and teachers think differently about writing and sharing students' writing.

Wordle

Wordle (www.wordle.net) calls itself "a toy" for creating "word clouds" from copied-and-pasted text. The clouds are a type of graphic artwork that can help students think in new ways about words, their meanings, and their importance. The website allows users to create a visual representation of text, making the words that appear more often larger and introducing color. Figure 3.2 is a Wordle that I created from the words of FDR's "Day of Infamy" speech (www.archives.gov/education/lessons/day-of-infamy).

Figure 3.2: "Day of Infamy" Wordle.

Other Wordle possibilities include:

- ☐ Pasting a student's text into Wordle and looking for over-used words

- ☐ Copying a lesson summary from a digital textbook into Wordle and starting the lesson by asking students to look for themes

- ☐ Using a Wordle to help students look for key vocabulary words

- ☐ Using a Wordle to help students express their feelings

- ☐ Encouraging students to write "about me" Wordle poems

Wikis and Writing

Previously, I discussed using wikis. This technology allows multiple users to compose, edit, and view documents, making this Web 2.0 tool particularly well suited to writing instruction. Permission settings can allow open access or limit access to a select class, committee, or group. The permissions can change depending on the collaboration needs.

Once the wiki is established, text pages can be added with a click of a button. Most wikis also have a discussion feature that allows threaded discussions about content. And there is no reason to worry if someone accidentally deletes the entire working document because a revision history records every action, and any such problems can immediately be solved. This revision history also allows the teacher and other users to see who is participating in writing and editing the document.

Wikis can allow students to participate in a variety of writing and editing interactions, such as:

Literature circles

Research collaborations

Question-and-answer sessions

Problems of the day

Character studies

Peer editing

Book talks

Pen pal collaborations

Getting started creating a wiki is an easy and inexpensive (sometimes free!) process. If a school district does not already offer wiki space, there are a number of online wiki sites friendly to education. Wikispaces (www.wikispaces.com) is the site I use to host my own wiki. This site offers free K–12 classroom wikis to educators. Teachers who sign up for a classroom wiki should be certain to select the "educator" link, as this will remove any ads from the classroom pages.

Another wiki service is PBworks (http://pbworks.com). Like Wikispaces, this website is friendly to educators, offering free wiki space. Both sites offer a number of template backgrounds from which to select and thus enhance the ability to individualize the look of the wiki.

Maintaining Focus

At the start of this chapter, I suggested that merely outfitting schools with technological "stuff" will not transform teaching and learning. Technology is here to stay, and the nature of technology—hardware, software, Web 2.0, and other online possibilities—is ever changing. Every teacher needs to engage in professional development to learn how best to use emerging technologies. But the bottom line is not technology. It is a focus on teaching and learning.

New technology brings possibilities for increased student engagement and active learning. But without a commitment to planning and delivering effective instruction—regardless of the technology—there will be no significant increase in student achievement.

Pen and paper, as "primitive" technology, or even a computer word-processing program, are not the real focus of writing. Educators and students must understand that Web 2.0 technology is not an end but simply an avenue that teachers and learners can take in their pursuit of new knowledge and understanding.

This point is extremely important and so is worth continuing. In the next chapter, I explore some additional technological tools and strategies designed to help teachers rethink how they structure lessons to maximize student engagement and active learning.

chapter 4

Developing a Digital-Rich Curriculum

When digital resources are incorporated in the curriculum, the possibilities are limited only by imagination—and funding, policies, and other real-life considerations, of course. However, there are many high-tech, low-cost technological tools that can be incorporated in traditional classrooms to transform them into technologically rich, innovative environments that support and encourage active learning.

With minimal investment and training, teachers can take students on a virtual magic-carpet ride around the globe, using sophisticated but free and easy-to-use Google Maps and Google Earth software. Teachers can help their students interact with classes on the other side of the world by using Skype. And teachers can help their students design 3-D cities of the future with Google SketchUp. These programs are used in many schools, and many students already know how to use them from activities they have done at home.

In this chapter, I will showcase some additional technological tools—many using Web 2.0 technology—that offer new possibilities for enriching teachers' instructional toolboxes of digital resources. I'm not talking about add-ons. Rather, these resources are to be woven into the curriculum, replacing traditional paper-and-pencil activities and stand-and-deliver teaching. In fact, teaching today would be difficult for me without some of these technological tools.

And the best part is that most of the digital resources included in this chapter require little beyond what is now normally available in most schools: a computer, high-speed access to the Internet, an LCD projector, and audio speakers.

Rethinking Curriculum Planning

I am convinced that all teachers can be a source of change for their students, colleagues with whom they collaborate, and even the leaders who support them. Business blogger Seth Godin (2008), author of ten international best-selling books, is an expert on the effects of social media. He has written,

> The first thing you need to know is that individuals have far more power than ever before in history. One person can change an industry. One person can declare war. One person can reinvent science or politics or technology. The second thing you need to know is that the only thing holding you back from becoming the kind of person who changes things is this: lack of faith. Faith that you can do it. Faith that it's worth doing. Faith that failure won't destroy you. (p. 71)

Each teacher must be a force for change, and each has the potential to be a leader by exposing colleagues to new ideas and technologies and supporting efforts to incorporate them in curriculum.

Fundamentally changing the curriculum will be difficult, and few school systems have the capacity to accomplish it with the urgency that is needed. According to Godin (2008),

> Our culture works hard to prevent change. We have long had systems and organizations and standards designed to dissuade people from challenging the status quo. We enforce our systems and call whoever is crazy enough to challenge them a heretic. And society enforces the standards by burning its heretics at the stake, either literally or figuratively. (p. 71)

With a master's degree in curriculum and a teaching career that spans more than twenty-five years, I have served on many curriculum committees. I have found that they often turn into textbook-adoption committees. However, planning curricula and adopting textbooks are two very different tasks, and they should be kept separate. A textbook is a tool—as is technology—for *delivering* a curriculum; the textbook should not *define* the curriculum.

In the previous chapter, I touched on standards, which should be the engines of any curriculum. Alignment to appropriate national, state or provincial, and local standards is a goal of curriculum planning, with the idea that alignment is a means of ensuring a focused pathway to success for all students. Unfortunately, curriculum documents too often die on the back shelf, collecting dust for years, unread, unrevised, and—in the view of busy teachers—unhelpful.

With the advent of the digital age, the opportunity has come to make curriculum guides living documents, though that has not yet happened universally. Moving curriculum documents from paper and binders to searchable digital resources capable of continuous updating and accessible 24/7 would not be a huge technological leap. But it would be a leap forward toward the full realization of a contemporary, relevant curriculum in which technology is integral, rather than an add-on.

Currently, most school districts that have digital networks only have space on the network for staff members and students to save their documents. This is a great first step, as data should be backed up on the network every night. However, that only addresses the minimum needs. What about collaborative sharing? My experience is that only a few districts provide for this activity at all, and very few share resources across grade levels and departments. Even fewer districts share resources outside the district.

A new generation of teachers, who have grown up collaborating and using social media, has entered the teaching ranks, and they need to be given permission to help change the education system. Tapscott and Williams (2006) have pointed out,

> If there is one overarching principle that defines what the new Web is, it's that we are building this thing together—one blog post, podcast, and mash-up after another. The Web is no longer about idly surfing and passively reading, listening, or watching. It's about peering: sharing, socializing, collaborating,

and, most of all, creating within loosely connected communities. (p. 45)

With this digital shift in mind, a hyperlinked curriculum, for example, would allow educators more flexibility to differentiate instruction and meet the needs of individual students. A digitally organized curriculum would enable teachers to search for the information they need, and ready access would make planning lessons that are fully aligned to standards easier and more accurate. Digital resources and reference media incorporated in such a hyperlinked curriculum would give teachers a wealth of instructional tools, including multimedia, images, activities, and other resources—far more than can be contained in a textbook. This is a new world of exciting possibilities, allowing all educators to rethink curriculum and instruction.

The future is here today for some educators, as institutions and individuals already are sharing curricula in new ways. For example, iTunes U (www.apple.com/education/itunes-u) is accessed through iTunes software that is free to download and works on both a Mac and a PC. iTunes describes iTunes U as "a powerful distribution system for everything from lectures to language lessons, films to labs, audiobooks to tours."

This mobile learning tool offers a growing collection of educational podcasts on topics as diverse as studying climate change, learning Japanese, or auditing a chemistry class at Oxford. Teachers are able to use these free podcasts to differentiate instruction and to extend learning beyond the classroom.

The educational possibilities of a digital curriculum are virtually infinite. There is so much information available on the Internet that it seems like a daunting task even to begin to collect and organize resources. Technology has given education the possibility of a truly open curriculum. An open curriculum can have many authors and collaborators instead of a single textbook source. It is not static. It is dynamic and constantly evolving because it can be changed.

The sense that, collectively, we are better, smarter, faster, or more knowledgeable than we are individually drives the development of many Web 2.0 tools. Wikipedia is a good example of experts coming together to share their passions and knowledge with the world. Each contributor to Wikipedia adds to our collective knowledge. Contributors check each other's work, combing out errors and sharing what they know.

In Illinois, where I live, the legislature passed an Internet Safety Law in 2009. (For further information on this law and its implications for the classroom, consult the Educational Technology section of the Illinois State Board of Education website, www.isbe .state.il.us/curriculum/html/internet_safety.htm.) This law identifies seven strands that need to be in the school curriculum and mandates that this type of curriculum be implemented statewide. There are more than nine hundred school districts in Illinois, all of which work largely in isolation. One leading school district in the southern tip of the state, however, created an amazing curriculum, linking the myriad of free online resources that included links to reproducible worksheets, educational videos, and lesson plans for teachers. They hyperlinked and digitally organized the resources, added various grade-appropriate examples, and then, in the Web 2.0 spirit, posted the digital curriculum on the state website to allow other school districts to access and modify it for local use.

In the past, the mandated Illinois curriculum probably would have been published in a binder and distributed throughout the state. There would have been little sharing of the curriculum (or subsequently identified resources) among neighboring districts. But now, because of the work of one team, schools and individual educators can save hours of work—and deliver instruction that not only aligns with state standards but also uses technological tools as integral resources to ensure active learning and encourage collaboration at all levels. This is an open, living curriculum.

Legal and Ethical Issues of Digital Sharing

Sharing and the idea of an open curriculum are embedded in NETS at all levels. However, with this new openness comes a number of issues related to law and ethics.

The Illinois faculty that created its open curriculum and shared it on the Internet is still the owner of that work—by default the copyright holder, whether a copyright notice is attached to the work or not. It would be neither ethical nor legal to republish that work without including clear attribution to the creators. But there are no prohibitions concerning using it, adapting it to local needs, adding to it, and sharing it further with others. That freedom was made specific by the developers of the curriculum.

This type of sharing is the spirit behind the Creative Commons licensing that I discussed earlier. Creative Commons essentially says that an individual or group may use another person's work, if it is so licensed, and mash it up—in other words, transform it in some way. The new user, however, cannot make a profit from doing so. Just as students need to know the boundaries of creative sharing, so, too, must teachers and administrators be aware of the legal and ethical constraints that come with digital sharing of any type.

For example, teachers should make sure when they are making their end-of-the-year CD or DVD for students that they do not insert full-length songs because, when multiple copies are burned for the students, this is likely a violation of copyright.

More Tools for a Digital Curriculum

Many possibilities unfold when teachers begin to think of curriculum in a digital form instead of traditional pencil-and-paper activities and assignments. Digital textbooks are just one of the possible vehicles for instruction. Many of the recently released textbooks have digital companions filled with animations, graphics, and interactive lessons. However, access to the online editions may be a problem if students do not have access to high-speed Internet at home.

A number of options will be explored in this chapter. In addition to digital textbooks, there are many online resources, including the computation website Wolfram Alpha. Additional free tools by Google will be investigated as they relate to curriculum, including Google Earth and Google SketchUp.

When discussing a digital curriculum, the power of video cannot be overlooked. I will explore the possibilities of YouTube in the classroom as well as additional video hosting sites.

There would not be a complete digital curriculum without seamless and ongoing assessment, so I have also included specific strategies for changing instructional practice.

Digital Textbooks

Traditional textbooks are a good way to illustrate the need for change to a digital-rich curriculum. They often are expensive, a cost that school districts pass on to parents and taxpayers in various ways, depending on the state, province, or local community. Because so much content is covered, many textbooks are large and heavy, especially for younger students. They also are inaccurate in some cases. And the textbooks in many subjects become outdated before they can be traded for newer editions because of lengthy adoption cycles—six, eight, or ten years are not unusual.

Increasingly, digital textbooks are becoming available for a fee, and there are many open-source textbooks free to download from the Internet. When something is licensed under open source, it means that the license shall not restrict any party from selling or giving away the content. Most such books are available through websites that can be accessed from any Internet-capable device.

Many school districts are looking closely at digital textbooks as they move toward one laptop to every child and wireless capabilities across the campus. One such school is La Grange Highlands Middle School in La Grange, Illinois. Rather than a backpack filled with heavy textbooks, students sling a laptop carry case across their shoulders. As the district is adopting new textbooks, they are looking closely at the interactivity in the digital companions. The 24/7 access has rescued many a struggling student who was unable to remember a difficult math concept. By clicking on a link in the online textbook, students can view screencasts of demonstrations of math problems being solved with step-by-step explanations. From a parent's perspective, the digital textbooks have also saved many trips back to school to get a book that was left behind.

Digital textbooks offer advantages over print, such as in-depth search capability and multimedia content. Voice programs also are available to make most digital textbooks into talking books for students who are struggling readers or visually impaired. Hyperlinks to additional resources extend the content beyond the initial plat-form, and built-in management systems for teachers can stream-line assessment and make differentiated instruction easier to accomplish on a consistent basis.

However, not everyone welcomes digital textbooks with open arms. Some parents may serve as a roadblock to transitioning to the exclusive use of digital textbooks. Many parents still feel that they can manipulate a physical textbook better and more easily and quickly find what they are looking for. Also, according to Josh Catone (2009) of Mashable, many students at the higher educa-tion level are reluctant to select the electronic version of a text-book because the cost savings is not that dramatic and there is no set standard format that works on all devices.

Digital texts will not become a reality until states or provinces and districts change the textbook-adoption process. I often share my belief that no book should make the final cut for adoption until a curriculum committee has fully researched its companion online text. In order to comply with the Americans with Disabilities Act (ADA), every textbook published since 2006 must have a digi-tal companion, but the quality of the digital resources varies dra-matically. Many offer only basic documents in Adobe's portable document format, commonly called PDF, with no embedded mul-timedia. For a new generation of students, schools need to adopt a new generation of textbooks, which means that the quality of digital companions must be regarded as an important factor in any textbook adoption.

Universal use of digital textbooks may be a few years away, but are traditional textbooks really still needed? More and more dis-tricts are moving to what I call a "hyperlinked curriculum." Some teachers already are organizing resources for classes on websites or wikis but are still required by their districts to have a class text-book, even if it is rarely used. Eric Frank, who spent seven years with a publishing company selling textbooks, had this to say about textbooks in a *USA TODAY* article: "The current business model fails the students, the faculties and the authors." He went on to explain, "Students are used to having choices in what to buy; instead they're getting the same thing they got 50 years ago and paying a lot for it. Instructors have different teaching styles, but a one-size-fits-all cookie-cutter book never allows them to deliver it. The authors are getting paid less and less for their book" (Shkolnikova, 2008).

Districts that take the plunge and stop purchasing textbooks will have to help parents and the community in the transition. A textbook is familiar, comfortable, and expected. If parents are to be active participants in their children's learning, then they, too, must feel comfortable accessing digital resources.

One key concern is access. Portable computers are essential so that students can use them wherever they choose to study. But even low-end laptops may be too expensive for many students. However, newer, smaller, less expensive devices suitable for digital textbooks are rapidly coming onto the market. Some are the small-scale laptops, generically called netbooks, made by various companies—for example, HP and Dell. The latest additions to the marketplace are electronic book (ebook) readers. (Ebook readers are discussed further in chapter 5.)

Another concern is universal access to the Internet, which can be a significant problem in impoverished areas. I believe this will change as wireless networks expand to allow individuals within ever-larger geographic areas to go online with little or no cost. Some schools are opening up their computer labs before and after school to help those students who do not have Internet access at home. Also, many public libraries provide free, wireless Internet access. Some communities are looking at "cloud solutions," meaning that an entire area has high-speed Internet access which is funded in a variety of ways including corporate sponsors, community organizations, and grants.

Wolfram Alpha

I believe that the dependence on textbook-driven instruction will diminish as teachers develop standards-based curricula using a wide range of digital tools. When I started teaching, textbooks were one of the few resources available, and the textbook often *was* the curriculum. That no longer needs to be the case. Today, with the diverse resources of the Internet only a few mouse clicks away, a textbook is usually the last place I turn for ideas.

A website that will help me illustrate this point is Wolfram Alpha (www.wolframalpha.com). Following is how the website operators characterize this innovative resource:

> Today's Wolfram Alpha is the first step in an ambitious, long-term project to make all systematic knowledge immediately computable by anyone. Enter your question or calculation and Wolfram Alpha uses its built-in algorithms and a growing collection of data to compute the answer.

For example, if a student encounters a problem in math class, he or she can enter the problem on the website, and, depending on the problem, the website can walk the student through the process of arriving at a solution. The Wolfram Alpha website provides many examples of its functionality, which are organized by topic, such as mathematics, physics, and weather.

Google Again

In today's digital world, Google is ubiquitous. I rely heavily on tools such as Google Earth, Google SketchUp, and Google Maps as integral elements of teaching for engagement, collaboration, and active learning.

Some of these applications, for example, Google Earth and Google SketchUp, are software that must be downloaded and installed. This may present a problem if you work in a district that prohibits or discourages downloading additional software to school computers. If you do not have installation privileges, consult—or beg— the technology manager. These powerful applications are not large downloads, but when in use, they can overtask a network. Also, unfortunately, older computers may not be able to run these applications. Google Maps, by contrast, is an online resource that can be accessed on the Internet and does not have to be downloaded.

As discussed previously, these applications and many others can be used across the curriculum. In chapter 3, for example, I described a seventh-grade history assignment that involved tracing the route of the Lewis and Clark expedition using Google Earth. This powerhouse application is worth some further description.

I always recommend that groups of students work together when using Google Earth. Otherwise, the network may slow to a crawl. Implicit in its name, Google Earth is exactly what this application delivers. Teachers and students can take virtual trips anywhere around the world. And on any virtual tour, everyone can get off the bus, so to speak, and take a closer look. However, it should be borne in mind that some geographic regions can be seen at higher resolution than others. For example, many rural areas do not have the level of clarity available in urban areas. And the satellite photos used to generate the Google Earth images are not in real time; in fact, they may be several years old.

The real power of Google Earth is to be found in the layers provided by the application. Geographic information can be overlaid one layer at a time or in multiple layers. For example, one of the layers is real-time weather. If students turn on that function, they will see whether it is raining or sunny in their target locale. Another layer is traffic flow, and so on. There are enough available layers that if too many are turned on at one time, it is hard to see the Earth.

Navigating in Google Earth is done by using sliders. For example, if students select a major city—say, Chicago—then they can slide in to look for places of interest, such as museums, monuments, historic sites, or parks. They can zoom down to street level, using "street view," and take a virtual stroll along Chicago's lakefront. Then, by clicking on a 3-D feature, students can watch Chicago's skyscrapers pop up from the map. So, without ever setting foot on a real tour bus, teachers can take their students on a virtual field trip nearly anywhere in the world.

The seventh-graders completing the Lewis and Clark assignment in chapter 3 inserted virtual pushpins to identify points of interest on the explorers' route. This feature, of course, can be used any-where in the Google Earth world, allowing students to add all sorts of information regarding the target locations. Advanced users can attach images, links, and videos to their pushpins, sequence them, organize them in an online folder, email them to a classmate, or post them on a wiki, a blog, or a website.

Google Earth has many features to explore, including:

A flight simulator

A sky map

A latitude and longitude grid

A sun tracker

A number of innovative teachers have already prepared curricular materials for Google Earth and have shared them on the Internet. Other teachers can find these materials—lesson plans, resource collections, and so forth—by searching the topic word(s) with the letters *kmz* appended to it. (The letters stand for "keyhole markup zip.") For example, an earth science teacher might use the words "erosion kmz" to initiate a search for curricular materials using Google Earth that other teachers have posted regarding erosion. This activity exemplifies the digital curriculum that I described previously.

Google SketchUp (described in chapter 2) complements Google Earth, allowing students to create 3-D models, for example, of the locales they visit on virtual tours. This program also can be used in other contexts. For instance, students might build replicas of scenes from a novel or a history book.

Google Maps, while not as complex as Google Earth, provides some of the same functions. Students can "visit" locations around the world and examine area maps, topography, and satellite views of communities. A street-view feature also allows students to "walk" some of the neighborhoods they visit.

Google Maps also allows students to create their own maps and provides a directory of maps created by others. These maps are located under a "My Maps" link; however, teachers should be aware that not all of the shared maps are appropriate for students. However, most tie in localized data, such as earthquake information, crime statistics, hiking trails, and so on.

The Video Revolution

Video consumption, creation, and sharing are big parts of the Web 2.0 revolution. We are living in an era defined by YouTube (www .youtube.com). In fact, the current generation of students is sometimes called the YouTube generation, raised on multimedia and now both producers and consumers.

YouTube was created in the mid-1990s by a small team working above a pizza parlor in California, where they unlocked the secret of compressing large video files and making them easy to view through a high-speed Internet connection. By 2006, the concept was such a success that YouTube was bought by Google for $1.65 billion (Helft & Richtel, 2006).

So, how does YouTube fit into the development of a digital-rich curriculum? In chapter 3, I introduced YouTube and a couple of related, YouTube-like websites (TeacherTube and SchoolTube.com), citing their potential for sharing students' work. But video of all sorts has much broader applications for curriculum and instruction.

YouTube should be available to teachers because it is a huge repository of content related to curricula in all areas. In some districts, however, YouTube is off limits even to teachers because the website is largely uncensored, and some content may not be appropriate for all students. This really boils down to a trust issue and treating educators as responsible, intelligent professionals. District and school leaders need to trust teachers to preview YouTube content that they plan to use for instruction. From my vantage point, if you cannot trust teachers to use YouTube appropriately, then you should not trust them to teach. Protecting students from inappropriate content is important, but it should not be an excuse for limiting teaching and learning options.

A quick search of the YouTube website finds many videos that present, supplement, or enhance content-learning opportunities— all with potential for increasing student engagement. Following are a few topic samples:

- ☐ Cells

- ☐ Volcanoes

☐ Geometry

☐ Education

☐ Reading

☐ Science

In addition to concerns about the appropriateness of some videos available on the Internet, there is the practical issue of bandwidth limitations. Simply put, bandwidth is like a hose that brings data into the school or district. Low bandwidth is like a garden hose; high bandwidth is like a fire hose. Districts need the fire hose because streaming video requires considerable bandwidth as it flows through the network.

Unfortunately, bandwidth is not a low-cost commodity. Schools and districts need to budget for high bandwidth in order to have the capacity to build fully functional digital curricula. In the meantime, however, many schools block streaming media, which also includes online radio, music, and RSS feeds. (RSS stands for "really simple syndication" and is a web-feed function for streaming radio, news headlines, blog posts, and so forth.) Blocking protects bandwidth capacity and network infrastructure, but it also blocks teaching and learning with streaming media.

Planning for Seamless Assessment

Integral to developing a digital-rich curriculum is planning for assessment that is both formative and summative. "Seamlessness" implies that assessment is fully incorporated in unit and lesson structures and is aligned, like the content, to local, state or provincial, and national standards. In order to achieve this end, a variety of assessment approaches need to be employed. Variety is essential because assessment should match content and teaching. Projects are individual, often differentiated for various students' needs, and include many types of strategies and instructional tools.

Formative assessment is particularly important for keeping active learning on target and ensuring that all students are making anticipated progress. In fact, in this era of high-stakes testing, ongoing formative assessment is doubly important. A high-stakes, summative, make-or-break final exam or term paper simply will not suffice.

One type of formative assessment in the spirit of a digital-rich curriculum is the use of student-created videos. Moviemaking projects are a great way to check for comprehension. When students make their own videos, they really are engaging in teaching. It is a truism that when we teach others, we also learn more effectively ourselves. Consequently, the process of making videos is engaged, collaborative, very active learning; and the video products serve as formative assessments that let teachers know what and how well students have learned.

A couple of examples are illustrative. They involve graduate students, but the principles are applicable from elementary school onward. One of my graduate students, a high school science teacher, found a song by the group Science Groove (www .science-groove.org), which boasts an extensive collection of science and math songs in their database. Science Groove had recorded a song about glucose to the tune of "Sugar, Sugar," by the Archies. The teacher searched for images that matched the words and used Windows Movie Maker to time everything. The images and the rewritten lyrics really helped students understand some difficult science concepts and to remember the vocabulary. I think this teacher's students will be tapping their toes and remembering this content for years to come.

Recently, I created a new group project to wrap up a weeklong graduate class with experienced teachers. Their assignment was to showcase five Web 2.0 tools they had learned during the week. Each group project was required to be some sort of presentation— and it had to be funny. This assignment could be my all-time favorite. The range of projects was broad and delightful: sing-alongs, lyrics rewritten and sung as a video soundtrack to still and moving images, mashups made using video clips, and so on. Without fail, every group created something funny. Many of the clips incorporated some of the funny moments from the class, poking fun at me or our less-than-optimal accommodations.

In weeklong classes like this one, I try to model what teaching and learning can look like when teachers use the wide range of Web 2.0 tools available to them. The adult participants' active learning goes hand in hand with deep engagement and collaboration. And that is exactly what should be happening at all levels in all schools.

chapter 5

Must-Have Technology for the Ideal Classroom

With all of the possibilities for instructional technology that I have discussed to this point, how do teachers and administrators sort out the must-haves from the nice-but-nonessentials? In this chapter, I explore the technological tools that ideally no classroom should be without.

Policy Lead-Ins

The full integration of Web 2.0 and other technological tools in digital-rich curriculum and instruction must be built from a tech-savvy policy base. Four factors figure prominently: permission, expectations, funding, and ongoing commitment. I have touched on the first of these in previous chapters.

School boards and administrators are the authorities that either facilitate technological innovation and integration or block them. To create a digital-rich curriculum and classrooms in which integrated technology supports and enhances engagement and collaboration, school authorities must permit teachers to use available technological tools.

Hand in hand with permission to incorporate technology in curriculum and instruction are the paired expectations that teachers will learn about and use the technological tools provided. This is the second factor. These expectations find grounding in the National Educational Technology Standards for Teachers (NETS-T), which also includes performance indicators (www.iste.org/Content/

NavigationMenu/NETS/ForTeachers/2008Standards/NETS_T_
Standards_Final.pdf). This document parallels NETS-S, which was
previously discussed. Another parallel is professional development for principals and instructional supervisors, so that they can
be fully supportive of teachers' efforts. Such professional development also is a necessary expectation.

Funding is the third issue. I spent more than five years on my local
school board, and so I understand school budgets and finance.
Even in times of shrinking education budgets, there are many
creative ways to fund technology, which I will suggest at various
points in this chapter in conjunction with specific types of technological tools. In our local school district, we have made major
strides in technology placement even as budgets have been
slashed. I firmly believe that certain technological tools need to be
standard in all classrooms. Every child deserves the opportunity to
learn with these powerful technologies.

Every teacher should be provided continuing professional development as new technological tools emerge and ongoing technical
support to ensure appropriate use of Web 2.0 and other tools. Both
types of support ensure that optimal tools are always functional
and available. This is the fourth factor: ongoing commitment from
district-level and building-based leaders to support technology
integration—with a substantial investment in professional development, which I will take up in chapter 7.

Vision and Collaboration

Designing the ideal classroom is much more than installing hardware and software. The policy factors I discussed derive from my
own guiding vision of a systemic, long-term transformation of
teaching and learning.

Just as learning often succeeds best when it is collaborative, so,
too, will the ideal classroom be more likely to become reality if
all of the school stakeholders are involved. School board members,
curriculum developers, administrators, teachers, parents, students,
and the community at large compose this stakeholder group. They
all will play a role in creating digital-rich classrooms.

The school board and the community at large must define the guiding vision. Deliberation may be prodded through a grassroots effort initiated by tech-savvy teachers, for example, or it may be an initiative originating from the board. However it comes about, once it is defined, the vision must be shared with all stakeholders.

Teachers are among the most important of the stakeholders, and they are the focus (along with students) of this book. But parents should not be overlooked. Truly transformed classrooms look and feel different from traditional classrooms, and some parents initially may be uncomfortable with the new approaches and with many of the forms of technology being proposed. Care needs to be taken to bring parents into the big picture. My experience has been that parents want their children to be excited about going to school and learning. Engaged, enthusiastic students can sell the transformation from traditional to technologically enriched classrooms.

Equipping the Ideal Classroom

In a fully functional, digital-rich classroom, the technology that is integral in curriculum and instruction will be readily accessible without checking it out or moving it from some other location. Certain high-end, seldom-used hardware might reasonably be available on a shared basis. But the basics for our ideal classroom should be in the classroom, not somewhere else. Availability is not only an issue during delivery of instruction but also in effective planning (pre-instruction) and evaluation (post-instruction). This availability applies to students as well as teachers. Many schools still use the model of a stand-alone computer lab that must be reserved for students' use weeks or months in advance, limiting flexibility in teaching and learning. This is not compatible with our ideal.

The ideal classroom in this illustration is a general classroom, the type of classroom most common to schools at all levels. Other specialized classroom spaces exist, of course, from art and music rooms to science labs, auto shops, and so on. Basic technological tools are needed in these spaces, but specialized classrooms also require specialized tools that are beyond the scope of this illustration. Also, in most cases, I avoid recommending particular hardware or software brands, except when a technological tool is uniquely associated with a brand, such as Apple's iPod touch. The only word of caution I would include about implementing the ideal in real classrooms is that it will be important to manage compatibility issues among various elements of both hardware and software.

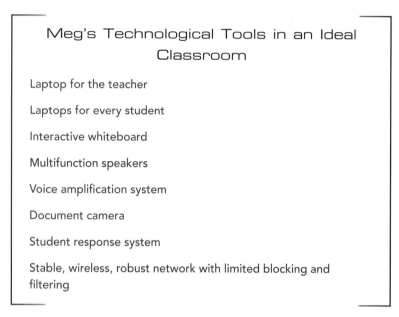

Meg's Technological Tools in an Ideal Classroom

Laptop for the teacher

Laptops for every student

Interactive whiteboard

Multifunction speakers

Voice amplification system

Document camera

Student response system

Stable, wireless, robust network with limited blocking and filtering

A Laptop for the Teacher

Every teacher needs to be issued an up-to-date laptop computer accessible 24/7, including throughout the summer. These computers may vary in power and software, depending on the specific needs of the teacher. For example, a high-technology user will need a more powerful computer than a teacher who makes less use of computer technology. The important point is that teachers need full access to these computers. As they try new Web 2.0 tools, they also will need the ability to install software and to modify their computers.

While the platform (PC or Mac) is a factor, whichever direction a district goes, the teachers' computers should be as powerful as the budget will allow. Many districts are electing to purchase wireless laptops and support a wireless network throughout the district or at least within the individual schools. Collateral components include carrying bags or cases and flash drives for backing up files and transporting them.

Tablet computers can be an excellent option. A tablet is a laptop with a display screen that swivels. It comes with preloaded software and a digital pen that allows users to draw or write directly on the display screen. Software captures this input and saves it. Using the tablet and a wireless projector, a teacher can walk around the room while teaching and hand the tablet to a student, for instance, to demonstrate how to solve a math problem. Tablet computers are effective tools, especially in math, science, art, and elementary classrooms.

A lower-cost tool is the new generation of netbooks, smaller laptop computers that are about half the size of a standard laptop. Netbooks have gained some popularity in education, mainly because of their compact size, six-plus hours of battery life, and relatively low sticker price. A number of current models cost less than $300 apiece.

Laptops for Every Student

In my ideal classroom, every student would be assigned his or her own laptop, accessible 24/7. Today's student-purposed laptops cost little more than high-end textbooks. Some schools already are going in this direction.

Laptops wirelessly connected to the Internet will stimulate certain changes in instruction. From teaching in this type of environment almost daily, I have learned to balance activities on the computer and off. There are "lids down" times so that group discussions can take place or students can work individually without the computer.

In schools that cannot make the leap to individual student laptops all at once, there are some steps that can be taken along the way to this goal. For example, the first step might be to start with laptops assigned to teachers, and the next step would be to put projectors in classrooms. Another lower cost option would be to explore the use of other types of devices such as the Apple iPod touch or iPad. A robust, networked computer lab might then be supplemented by multistation mini-labs of, say, five computers in each classroom, with the classroom computers linked on the same network as the lab. Laptops, rather than desktops, would allow greater flexibility, both in classrooms and in the lab.

Computers on Wheels

Many districts are moving toward using COWS, or computers on wheels. A COW is better than having no access, but usually each COW unit is expected to be shared. Districts or schools considering the COW route should consider the following factors:

Cost

Mobility

Security and safety

Storage (central and classroom)

Checkout procedures

Scheduling

Sharing partners

Electrical power needs

If I were designing—or redesigning—a school building today, I would focus on creating flexible learning spaces and providing as much student access to technology as possible. Since redesign is most likely, one phase-in initiative could be to provide individual student laptops to one grade at a time—at the same time, focusing on intensive professional development and coaching for teachers of the affected grade.

An Interactive Whiteboard

An interactive whiteboard (IWB) connects to a computer through a USB port, and then what looks like a simple whiteboard becomes a computer screen that users can manipulate with their fingers or electromagnetic pens. You probably have seen these boards in use on television during news or weather broadcasts. Newer IWBs also have a projector that hangs above the board, thereby eliminating shadows and the need for additional calibration.

IWB software galleries come filled with many tools organized for teachers, everything from electronic protractors to interactive maps of all sorts. Galleries are constantly updated and can be customized, plus many teacher-created lessons using interactive whiteboards can be found on the Internet.

The licensing for most of the IWB software also allows it to be loaded on other computers. Having the software on the student computers, for example, allows students to work on their own, planning and creating projects using these powerful tools.

A recording feature of the IWB can be used to create a video that captures an entire lesson—every move on the board—along with the users' voices. Such videos then can be uploaded to a teacher's website, for example, to share with students who were absent for the lesson or for general review. All of these features are especially useful in classes for students with diverse needs because IWBs encourage intense interactivity.

IWBs do not work well as shared technology. Mobile units are available, but I do not recommend them because every time they are moved, they need to be recalibrated. If a building can provide only a mobile setup, I would advise mounting it in a single room—creating an IWB lab in essence—rather than actually moving it from place to place. The projector, if used, should be mounted on the ceiling. It has to be mounted with precision to ensure that the projected image exactly fits the board. Permanent mounting of the system makes it much easier to use the IWB effectively.

Multifunction Speakers

In order to make the most of multimedia resources, the ideal classroom should be equipped with high-quality, multifunction speakers. Many IWB manufacturers, for instance, offer optional speakers that mount next to the board. These speakers are powerful and reduce the number of cords that need to be plugged in to the computer.

Sound design should be part of any plan for an ideal classroom. Speakers need to be multifunctional because there are many sound resources that teachers can use. For example, I coached a math teacher who wanted to increase engagement in his classroom. One of his strategies was to embed various sounds in his lessons. He downloaded sound clips of all sorts and "hid" them in the lessons. Later, he built a gallery of multimedia resources. Now, he can start almost any lesson by playing a quick audio or video clip, which immediately engages his students.

Music, sound effects, and short video clips—all can help engage learners. But such tools are ineffective without good sound. Other options include portable speakers. I often use my iPod speakers to project sound. Whatever the solution, every classroom needs good sound.

A Voice Amplification System

Many schools are noisy environments in which students are easily distracted. A classroom voice amplification system can help overcome the noise by amplifying the teacher's voice. In my experience, classrooms outfitted with these systems feel different from other classrooms; students are calmer and more focused. Such systems also have been used successfully with hearing-impaired students and students with certain learning disabilities, but now more schools are installing them in all classrooms as a way to increase engagement.

Most classroom systems include a small lavalier or lapel-type microphone for the teacher and one or more classroom microphones—all wireless in most cases. Students can use the classroom microphones when they present reports or perform skits. Various classrooms in a school will use different channels to avoid overlap with other classroom systems.

A Document Camera

A document camera connects to a computer. Documents can be placed under the camera and projected onto a screen. These technologically advanced devices update the concept of the opaque projector; they are useful for showing more than simply flat documents, such as student compositions, maps, illustrations, and so forth. If it will fit under the camera, it can be projected for the whole class to see—a dissected frog, a science experiment, artifacts, and other objects.

Many document cameras also can serve as webcams (cameras that broadcast over the Internet), making it possible to use the document camera with a web application such as Skype. The camera software also may record, allowing for the later viewing or analysis of a segment, such as a skit.

A friend who teaches art tells me that she cannot teach without her document camera. Before she had the document camera, she would have to bring everyone up around the front table to see a demonstration, which made it difficult for some students to see well. Using the camera, she can demonstrate art techniques that all of the students can see from their seats. She also can show sample artworks and share images from her large collection of art books. With a click of the button, she can also snap a picture of whatever the camera sees and then email it or use it in another application.

A Student Response System

Student response systems were extensively described in chapter 2. Such a system should be part of the ideal classroom—to facilitate instantaneous formative assessment, to stimulate student participation, to maximize effective use of classroom time for routine data collection, and many other purposes.

A Stable, Wireless, Robust Network With Limited Blocking and Filtering

Working with various schools, I hear many stories about networks and the people who protect the networks. Often I find that the technology department functions independent of the other departments, making decisions to protect the network without considering the bigger picture that includes teaching and learning. I sometimes have to "translate" between the technicians and educators. A district's network and data should be protected, but excessive blocking and filtering limits learning opportunities for students and teachers alike. Balance is the goal, and that must be articulated by district officials and understood by the entire learning community.

Many sites contain inappropriate content that should be blocked. However, overly broad filtering protocols block innocuous or educationally valuable websites. Health sites, for example, sometimes are blocked because filtering is triggered by sex-related keywords (which the filter treats as pornography-related), making students' Internet research on valid health topics, such as breast cancer or sexually transmitted diseases, difficult if not impossible to accomplish.

Most filtering software can be "tiered" to filter various levels of content based on permissions granted to groups of users, such as classes by grade level. The appropriate tier of access is determined by the login of the user. For example, YouTube might be tiered as open to staff members but not to students. Filters also can be overridden if special access is needed to websites otherwise blocked. Overrides are not allowed in some districts; in others, override capability may be limited to certain individuals and override access may be time limited.

While no one advocates that students be allowed wholly unsupervised access, there is a case to be made for allowing teachers to be the monitors of students' Internet use, rather than arbitrary filtering software. After all, in many cases, when students leave the locked-down Internet environment of the schools, many go home to an unblocked Web.

A stable network is critical if teachers and students are to effectively and efficiently use the technology. An adequate budget for infrastructure development (including daily backup of files) is necessary for creating a stable network. Wireless capacity aids flexibility of use and reduces wire clutter (a potential safety hazard). And robustness refers to network capacity for multiple, simultaneous use without any substantial reduction in the speed of data transmission.

Desirable Technological Tools for Students

A number of additional technological tools are desirable for educational purposes but not yet essential—though they may well be the must-haves of the future.

Ebook Readers

The ebook reader market is booming. Various devices are available to allow users to read books electronically. Amazon's Kindle, for example, comes in a couple of sizes, has substantial capacity to hold a large number of downloaded books, and supports other handy features, such as bookmarks and note-taking. Thousands of books are available, and most are considerably lower in price than their paper counterparts.

The Sony Reader and the Barnes & Noble nook are other recent entries. There are ebook reader apps for Apple's iPhone and iPod touch (and the iPod touch's big brother, the iPad). Future developments are likely to include greater cross-platform availability.

iPod Touch or iPad Devices

More versatile than stand-alone ebook readers, Apple's iPod touch and larger iPad devices offer app-based ebook readers as well as a number of other applications that would be useful in the classroom, among them:

- ☐ Calendar
- ☐ Calculator
- ☐ Notepad
- ☐ Email
- ☐ Music

Wireless Slates

Wireless slates are like individualized interactive whiteboards. Slates are different from the student laptop computers discussed earlier in this chapter. The wireless slate enables the teacher to walk around the room and still manipulate the computer that is projecting the image on the screen to the whole class. An example is the SMART slate (www.smarttech.com). Such devices can enhance engagement and collaboration.

From Dreams to Reality

It is easy to dream about the technological tools for the classrooms of the Web 2.0 generation, but such dreams must become reality if we truly want to transform teaching and learning. Every child deserves to learn in this type of environment. Every teacher deserves a chance to see how these tools could invigorate his or her teaching.

As I stated at the start of this chapter, however, the ideal classroom cannot be defined merely by a list of must-have technology. It must be defined by a clear vision of effective schooling, arrived at collaboratively by those invested in education and the future of our children.

chapter 6

Web 2.0 Classroom: A Virtual Field Trip

When teachers teach for active learning, the effects are felt not only by their own students, but also by other teachers and students, administrators, and parents. In making the most of Web 2.0 tools and related technology, teachers empower students to direct their own learning. As I have pointed out in the preceding chapters, teaching for active learning in this fashion requires teachers to plan curriculum and instruction in new ways. They also must actively communicate with colleagues, administrators, and parents so that unfamiliar approaches in the classroom can be understood and embraced.

In this chapter, we will take a virtual field trip to an active-learning fifth-grade classroom. I will share observations about this energetic learning space and the various roles taken by the teacher and her students. In particular, I will direct attention to several pertinent factors that build success for all students in this classroom, including students' on-task behaviors, the teacher's actions, feedback from the building administrator and parents, and the teacher's planning strategies, along with the Web 2.0 tools she uses in her classroom.

Snapshot of Active Learning

During a professional development session with a group of teachers, I had the opportunity to take them to visit a classroom in which the teacher and her students truly have embraced active learning. That actual field trip is the basis of our virtual field trip.

The teacher's name is Nicole. She is a risk-taker—creative, organized, and energetic. In professional development sessions, she is like a sponge, absorbing everything and returning to her classroom eager to try new approaches. Prior to the teachers' field trip, I had spent several days with Nicole, teaching her new tools that she could take back to her classroom.

Our visit took place during the last two weeks of school, when many classes are winding down the year. However, this class was busy and on task, although at first glance some might have thought that it looked chaotic. Quite the contrary, this lesson was anything but disorganized; it actually was masterfully orchestrated.

The setting is a fifth-grade, self-contained classroom that is rather small given the thirty-four students assigned to this class. The students' desks are pushed together to form larger tables. The school is located in a lower socioeconomic area. This is an inclusive school in all ways. Bilingual students and students with special needs are mainstreamed in this classroom.

Nicole has been teaching about six years and working with the new technological equipment in her classroom about seven months. The new equipment includes an interactive whiteboard, a laptop for her use, a projector, speakers, Flip cameras, iPods, and some other technological tools. Nicole received a grant to purchase most of these tools, and the students mainly use free websites for Web 2.0 tools. The class also has access to a cart with student computers. The computer cart is shared with four other classrooms. On the day of our visit, the computer cart is available. However, along with its presence comes a sense of urgency, because another class needs the cart tomorrow.

The students are in literature circles, small groups with the task to summarize the book they have been reading. The objective is written on the board, and Nicole has already set clear expectations, including providing an assessment rubric for each group. But this is where the "sameness" ends. Every group—there are seven—is doing something different, based on each group's interests. Walking around the room and taking in the students' activities is exciting. None of the students is off task. In fact, most don't seem to notice the eight "extra teachers" in the room.

Group 1 is in a corner, listening to an audio version of the book. A class rule is that when earbuds are in their ears, students must use their fingers as they follow along in the print version of the book. Five pairs of earbuds are plugged in to a hub connected to an iPod. Everyone is on task. They are planning to create a podcast when they are finished summarizing the story. They will use Audacity (http://audacity.sourceforge.net), open-source recording and editing software, and a microphone. They tell us that they will do the recording in the hall, which they call their "recording studio."

Group 2 will create movies by using the class's Flip (www.theflip.com/en-us) camcorders and editing their work with the Flip software. These low-cost cameras are very easy to use and plug directly into the USB port of any computer with no additional cables to insert or software to install. The students are doing a mock interview with characters in the story.

Group 3 is creating Glogs, mashups using the website Glogster (www.glogster.com), with the summary information from the story. One student prints a sample design for us; the quality is amazing. The students also plan to add audio and video to their Glogs.

Group 4 has chosen VoiceThread (http://voicethread.com), a group discussion interface with multimedia, to create a media presentation. They are hoping to find other people who have read the book and ask them to comment on their favorite parts. This is the students' first time using VoiceThread, so they are struggling slightly.

Group 5 is at the interactive whiteboard, using the IWB software to create a presentation. They are accessing images from the gallery as well as searching online.

Group 6 is building their presentation around a cartoon character created by one of the boys in the group. This amazing piece of artwork was created in a simple paint program that comes preloaded in PCs running Microsoft Windows. We are astounded, so much so that we bump the group at the IWB temporarily so that the student can show us how he created the cartoon character.

Group 7 is creating a mashup in Windows Movie Maker. They have downloaded video clips from Discovery Streaming (http://

streaming.discoveryeducation.com), a subscription website comprised of professionally produced, informative video segments on a variety of topics. The students are discussing which segments to keep and how to sequence them.

All of the students are actively involved in some element of the various group projects, exhibiting real engagement and excitement. As each group finishes, the students publish their projects independently and upload everything to the classroom Moodle (http://moodle.org), a learning management tool. (I will further describe Moodle later in this chapter.)

I believe that every child should have the kinds of active-learning opportunities we observe. This classroom is rich in creativity and collaboration. It is well organized, and students have ready access to real-world tools.

Teacher as Tribe Leader

During our teachers' field trip, Nicole shared with us that she would go home that evening, put up her feet, comment electronically on her students' work, and assess whether they had successfully completed their various tasks. Nicole's comments will be accessible on the class Moodle site the next time the students log in from home, school, or the library—or maybe even from their phones.

After reading Seth Godin's book *Tribes* (2008), I reflected on the relevance of the tribe concept to schooling and thought about Nicole as a tribe leader. Nicole's leadership is what makes her classroom buzz with productive energy. During our visit, Nicole continually walked around the classroom, checking on students' progress, troubleshooting, and learning from her students.

Nicole is a smart tribe leader because she is taking the "guide on the side" role. She understands that she is not the font of all knowledge. Instead, her leadership style allows and encourages her students to learn from each other. When a problem is solved, the collective group gets wiser. According to Tomlinson (2001), "In a differentiated classroom, the teacher uses many different group configurations over time, and students experience many different working groups and arrangements. 'Fluid' is a good word to describe assignment of students to groups in such a heterogeneous classroom" (p. 3).

As tribe leader, Nicole knows to surround herself with other like-minded thinkers, both in her district and in the personal learning networks (often referred to as PLNs) in which she participates. At this time, Nicole is the only teacher in her school so fully engaged in Web 2.0–fueled active teaching and learning. But she participates in an extended teacher community through Skype, Twitter, Ning, and other networks, where she can be a member of a virtual team to share resources, ideas, and suggestions. This is tribe thinking. This is collaborative leading and learning.

The other teachers peppered Nicole with questions when we returned to our professional development session. For example, one teacher asked about the noise level in the room. Actually, the room was not as loud as one might expect. Nicole explained that if the noise bothers students and they are working independently, then they have permission to put in their earbuds. Nicole shared that this is the way that she has always taught; she is uncomfortable when students are quiet. Some of the other teachers seemed uneasy with this style of teaching, but they acknowledged that Nicole must be doing something right. Her students were demonstrably learning the skills detailed in NETS.

Another teacher asked about direct instruction. Nicole confirmed that there were times when she used direct instruction. Such times usually started with vocabulary of some type to activate schema about a topic. Nicole would gather the whole class together to check prior knowledge, clarify the objective of the lesson, and review essential vocabulary. Nicole also used a number of direct-instruction strategies during some lessons to check for comprehension. For instance, Nicole often used a student response system to gather data and to adjust the pace of a lesson.

What if Nicole didn't have the technology? By her account, she would not feel as though she could be as effective as a teacher without the technological tools she now uses to engage her students.

Nicole's Web 2.0 Tools

A few Web 2.0 tools that Nicole used merit special attention. Previously, several were mentioned in the context of her students' group work that have not been described in earlier chapters. Moodle, in particular, which is for whole-class use, may be new to many of you.

Audacity

Audacity (http://audacity.sourceforge.net) is free software that can be downloaded and used to record and edit audio files.

Flip

Flip (www.theflip.com/en-us) is a low-cost video camera that easily transfers video to the computer via the USB port.

Glogster

Glogster (www.glogster.com) is a website that allows students to mash up various media: video, audio, still images, text, animations, and graphics. This tool is online, and so there is no need to download and install software.

VoiceThread

VoiceThread (http://voicethread.com) is a free website for creating online multimedia presentations. This mashup site allows users to upload video, record audio, add still images, and create digital stories. Projects can remain public or be made private. For public projects, the makers can invite others to leave audio or text comments. Teachers are using this site in amazing ways. For example, some ask their students to do book talks and then to ask their parents to comment on them. Other students have done collaborative research reports about various states, working with students across the country who live in those states. Students in Taiwan who are learning English have shared poems with native speakers in the United States and elsewhere, who then added comments about the poems. The possibilities are limitless.

Moodle

Moodle (http://moodle.org), a course management system (CMS), is a free app that educators can use to create effective online learning sites. A teacher can post a classroom calendar, create discussion boards, post descriptions of upcoming events, upload assignments, and archive students' work. Teachers also can use Moodle for quizzes, wikis, databases, and chats. This open-source software is continually evolving and expanding to include new features.

Nicole's Planning Strategies

Since the interactive whiteboard was installed, Nicole has spent more time planning and less time grading papers. The software that came with the IWB is so powerful and has so many features that it took her some time to master the flow of the lessons. The up-front time is well spent, however. Once Nicole has prepared a lesson, the next time she teaches the concept, she will be ready. Nicole's collaborative nature makes her willing to share lessons with colleagues down the hall or around the globe. In turn, she can receive lessons from others that will fit her students' needs and interests. She does not always have to start from scratch.

Tomlinson (1999a) has suggested,

> During planning, a teacher should generate specific lists of what students should know (facts), understand (concepts and principles), and be able to do (skills) by the time the unit ends. Then the teacher should create a core of engaging activities that offer varied opportunities for learning the essentials she has outlined. These activities should lead a student to understand or make sense of key concepts and principles by using key skills. (p. 40)

Nicole always starts her lesson planning with a clear objective that is aligned to state standards. Then she plans for active learning by looking for ways to reduce direct instruction while covering the target content. This type of planning requires Nicole to gather ideas from various sources, in addition to coming up with her own ideas. She gathers much of her instructional repertoire online. There are countless lessons available on the Web in all curricular areas. Sifting through the available lessons and locating those appropriate for specific grade levels, however, takes some advanced searching skills. Nicole accesses a user-friendly search engine. A good example is the "advanced search" feature in Google (see sidebar).

Using Google's Advanced Search Feature

Mastering the advanced search feature can save hours of random searching. Here's how to do it. To start, look for the "exact phrase" text box and type in a short phrase to describe what you are searching for. The search will be done in the same word order as the phrase. For example, if you enter "rocks and minerals," the search engine will not find a website that lists "minerals and rocks." This strategy can eliminate unwanted results, but the phrasing must be done with care. Avoid words or phrases such as "activities" or "lesson plans" because they are too vague and will bring too many results.

The next most powerful option is the "without" box. I usually put in "Amazon Barnes Noble" because I don't want to buy anything; I just want to see what others have created.

Finally, knowing some of the common file extensions can help you sort out the most useful sites to examine. For example, a file name ending in .doc is a document. Here are a few others that are common:

.htm or .html (document with html coding that can be read by Internet browsers)

.jpg (image - Joint Photographic Experts Group)

.mov (QuickTime movie)

.ppt (PowerPoint presentation)

.wmv (Windows Media Video)

As Nicole surfs the Web and finds resources, she uses a clear on-screen filing system with folders to keep everything organized and in place. Tools, sites, and resources may change over time, but

Nicole will have many lessons planned, organized, and filed away for future use.

Another aspect of planning is monitoring student progress so that initial plans can be altered as students' needs change. How does Nicole know what everyone is doing? Nicole's students set weekly goals, and during the week, she checks these goals and confers with each student. She can give her students feedback at any time through the Moodle interface. Also through Moodle, Nicole can see exactly what students have submitted. On days when her class has the computer cart, very little paper is used. Nicole can create an assignment as an electronic document, and students can download the document, complete the assignment, save it to their network drive, and turn it in to Nicole through Moodle.

Reactions From Others

Today's students thrive in active-learning classrooms like Nicole's. Roger Schank (2002), distinguished professor of computer science at Carnegie Mellon University and known as one of the world's leading researchers in artificial intelligence, has said, "Education should be about preparation for living in today's world" (p. 8). Still, how have others reacted to Nicole's approach?

Administrators

Does Nicole get in trouble for teaching as she does? "No," she said, "my principal is very supportive because she sees the students engaged and thriving in this environment. She keeps her eyes open for professional development sessions for me, supports my grant writing, and helps me any way she can."

The International Society for Technology in Education (ISTE), along with creating standards for teachers, also developed National Educational Technology Standards (NETS) for administrators, which were updated in 2009 (www.iste.org/Content/NavigationMenu/NETS/ForAdministrators/NETS_for_Administrators.htm). The general message of NETS for administrators is that leadership needs to model the use of Web 2.0 tools and to support teachers as they are learning to make technology integral in teaching and learning.

Parents

Some parents have told Nicole that their children worry about transitioning to the middle school. The students are afraid that their new teachers will stand up and talk all period, and they will just have to take notes. They know that what they are experiencing with Nicole is different from what many students experience, and they want to continue to learn in this type of environment. Few parents question Nicole's digital-rich teaching. On the contrary, she receives a great deal of feedback about how excited students are about coming to school and how they continue to learn outside of school.

This experience was in a fifth-grade classroom, but the process could easily be replicated in classrooms at all levels. With older students, the projects could be much richer with curriculum connections to the real world.

chapter 7

Changing Professional Development

When I began my career teaching in an elementary school, my limited professional network consisted of the teachers in my building. By serving on various committees, I met a few other educators in other buildings in our relatively small district. Once or twice a year, teachers would come together for a professional development session, which usually was conducted in a large group with little or no interaction.

My professional network expanded slightly when I began to work on a master's degree in curriculum and instruction. Because I selected a cohort program in which a group of graduate students stays together for two years, my face-to-face professional network grew, but by only twenty people.

All of this took place about twenty-five years ago, and the options for professional growth beyond this limited collegiality were to read journals, attend workshops outside the district, talk with other teachers, and read books on education topics. When I entered the profession, I was fortunate to become part of a great team of teachers who worked well together, many of them veteran educators who had been in the district for years. I gained a measure of professional comfort when my colleagues would share how they taught this or that, but I also remember feeling isolated and expected to follow "the way we do this."

A few years into my career, I moved to a larger school district. The transition offered many new opportunities for personal and professional growth. I was assigned to a school with a dynamite principal who helped me find a professional growth path and direction as a teacher. My new, larger district also was rich in professional development opportunities, supported by a culture of professional sharing that helped me to grow as a teacher and later as a presenter. We teachers were expected to share strategies, to articulate ideas, and to collaborate across various curricular areas. Professional learning sessions were well structured; experts were brought in; and opportunities were plentiful. Still, communication beyond our face-to-face, in-district, or in-school sessions was limited to mail and phone calls in this era before even voicemail had become common. The only "technology" we had in the building was a ditto machine.

Things Have Changed

Today, in sharp contrast, many technological tools have been developed that can help educators grow professionally. For example, tuning in to professional conversations within one's school, across the district, or around the globe has never been easier. It is all about networking. The bottom line for today's educators is this: if you don't collaborate, you will not be successful in our modern, fast-paced world. I cannot overemphasize the importance of collaboration.

In their popular 2006 book *Wikinomics: How Mass Collaboration Changes Everything*, authors Don Tapscott and Anthony D. Williams illustrated how businesses today must collaborate or perish. I believe our job as educators is similarly situated; our "business" is to prepare students for the world in which they will be living and working—a world immersed in technology, much of it now dominated by Web 2.0.

During the summer, I teach weeklong graduate classes for teachers. This work keeps me fresh and pushes my technology expertise. The classes also represent a powerful professional development model, and what participants learn affects how they approach teaching and learning when they return to their classrooms. Many teachers take my classes summer after summer, learning new things every year.

One summer, I was teaching a group of young teachers. They were very tech savvy and could multitask like nothing I had ever seen. During this class, affectionately known as "tech camp," everyone works on a computer and is connected through a wireless network. This particular group all had their own laptops (or school-issued laptops). Because I model the importance of using social networks when teaching, I gave everyone permission to multitask. Off they went, Twittering, Facebooking, and Plurking. (Later in this chapter, I will describe Twitter, Facebook, and Plurk in some detail.) I found the resulting deep engagement truly fascinating.

They immediately started sharing what we were doing in tech camp with their network of other educators. Soon, whenever I shared a resource, the network would share something similar, and then one of the teacher participants in the class would add that newly acquired resource to our tech camp wiki (http://megormi .wikispaces.com/Camp2009). Networking participants also could tune in to the series of Twitter messages, organized using the hash tag "#camp09." A hash tag (also seen as one word, *hashtag*) is a device that allows Twitter users to search for posts (called "tweets") on a specific topic, in this case our tech camp.

Instead of a face-to-face group of twenty-six teachers, I now had a much larger audience, all sharing and collaborating on the topics being covered. And what was just as remarkable was that, for this group, it was a natural way to learn.

Looking back, if I had wanted to go to the next level technologically, I would have Ustreamed the class sessions. Ustream (www.ustream .tv), launched in 2007, is a live video-broadcasting platform, which would have allowed me to broadcast tech camp in real time and globally—literally to anyone with a computer and an Internet connection. I also might have tried screencasting class segments for later reference. Screencasting refers to capturing computer screen output (also called "video screen capture") and is software driven; one software version is Camtasia Studio (www.tech smith.com/camtasia.asp).

Text messaging during tech camp also helped us answer technical or curriculum-related questions, for example, about the best music to use for a variety of projects. We even used text messaging and the website Poll Everywhere (www.polleverywhere.com), described in chapter 2, as a follow-up after one class segment. We displayed the data on the class website.

All of these activities are possible with most modern computers, a little know-how, and some creative thinking. But the approach is a dramatic shift from traditional professional development, and that shift can seem intimidating. My hope is that this book will make that shift—both in professional learning and classroom instruction—less intimidating and more inviting.

Web 2.0 Tools Help Develop Networks

The World Wide Web is a trove of professional development ideas, information, and resources, but with it comes the risk of information overload. It is easy to get overwhelmed. I used to set up filters using a reader and RSS feeds to organize the flow of information. RSS basically is a connection to a blog or website through another website that is called a "reader." To read the selected blogs, a user logs in to a reader, and all of the blogs to which the user subscribes can be seen there. Examples of readers include Google Reader (www.google.com/reader), Bloglines (www.bloglines.com), and NewsGator (www.newsgator.com). RSS did the work of bringing me blog entries to keep me updated, but I still had to sift and synthesize all of the information. Most days, I would give up and work on something else.

Now, I have an established network that helps me stay current. Using various social media tools, the network in which I participate shares what we collectively know and have learned from each other. I learn much every day through collaboration and sharing—so much so that I miss the network whenever I am not connected for an extended time.

Earlier, I described networking by participants in tech camp as Twittering, Facebooking, and Plurking. Social networking is not new; we have been social networking all our lives. What we have with Web 2.0 tools are new platforms for social networking, providing us with new ways to collaborate.

Facebook

Facebook (www.facebook.com) was founded in February 2004, and it quickly swallowed up young adults at colleges and universities worldwide. At first, only those who could confirm a collegiate email address were allowed into this social network, making it an exclusive (and therefore more desirable) environment. Finally in September 2006, Facebook was opened to the world. According to the Facebook website, there are over 350 million active users as of this writing.

Facebook is a popular social networking site that allows people to make friends with other people, post images and text, and share various aspects of their lives. It has become so mainstream that corporations and other organizations are incorporating Facebook into their marketing strategies.

Plurk

Plurk (www.plurk.com) is a free micro-blogging service that allows registered users to send short messages to one another. Plurking is very much like Twittering, but the messages are displayed chronologically.

Twitter

Today it seems that the whole world is "atwitter." Twitter (http://twitter.com) is a social networking and micro-blogging platform that allows users to gather followers and post short messages. Tweets, or posts, are limited to 140 characters or fewer. This social network currently is my number-one source of professional growth. I like the character limitation because it makes for less sifting through wordy posts.

When I first began twittering, I thought it was a waste of time. But I stuck with it. As I built my network, I began to see the power of this tool to facilitate collaboration among busy people. Twitter is the vehicle, but the people in the network develop the content. Using Twitter as my personal learning platform helps me connect with experts and others who are passionate about the topics in which I am interested, without regard to our diverse geographic locations.

Many people begin on Twitter by "lurking," meaning that they are reading posts but not contributing to the network. Professional development really begins on Twitter when users contribute to the conversation.

Getting Started on Twitter

Set up a free account at Twitter (http://twitter.com) by, first, choosing a username and login password.

Second, complete your online profile. Many people read profiles to decide whether to include others in their network. Adding a photograph of yourself can help others in the network remember you.

Third, find people (sometimes called "tweeple" on Twitter) using the "find people" function. You can search by usernames (for example, mine is "megormi") or real names, if you know of others to whom you want to connect. Request to follow your selected individuals. Once they accept, you are connected. You will see their posts, and they will see yours.

Finally, grow your network by looking for people who would bring value to the conversations you are interested in having. As your network grows, you will see the power of collaborative conversation.

Twitter provides some built-in tools to help professional networks grow. One is "Mr. Tweet" (http://mrtweet.com), which provides recommendations of who to follow based on who already is in a given network. A number of other Twitter add-ons also are available, including:

☐ WeFollow (http://wefollow.com), a search aid to find people of interest

☐ Twitter4Teachers (http://twitter4teachers.pbworks.com), a wiki that helps make connections

☐ TweetDeck (www.tweetdeck.com/beta), an account organizer

☐ Seesmic (http://seesmic.com), a desktop organizer

☐ TwitPic (http://twitpic.com), an app for tweeting pictures

☐ SnapTweet (http://snaptweet.com), an app for sharing Flickr pictures on Twitter

A Professional Development Example

As a professional development specialist, I start every session that I conduct with a segment called "Let Me Show You What I Learned Yesterday." Doing this forces me to learn at least one new thing a day. It also means that my students always get the freshest ideas. I am bolstering the people in my networks, and in return, they feed me new ideas to try today and share tomorrow.

Professional development must be a personal undertaking, a commitment to embrace the notion of contributing to and drawing from the network. Professional development also can and should be organized by school leaders. District-supported, collective professional development is essential. Let's take a look at such an endeavor.

Recently, I worked with two talented educator teams in a middle school. These teachers were participants in a grant-funded project titled Enhancing Education Through Technology (EETT). The project provided technological tools for classrooms and extensive professional development. I was brought in to work with the participant groups, specifically to focus on redesigning lessons to maximize learning opportunities for all students.

The two groups were cohesive teams that already embraced collaborative planning and resource sharing. Both groups were composed of risk-takers, teachers willing to dive in and try new things. School leaders also set high expectations and created a culture of collaboration, which was evident in a variety of ways, including administrative scheduling of a joint planning period each day for the teams. During their planning time, the team members shared what they were doing. They engaged in collaborative brainstorming and troubleshooting. Working together, the teachers accomplished much more than they could as individuals.

The grant provided equipment for each project participant's classroom, including:

- ☐ Laptop for the teacher

- ☐ Interactive whiteboard with speakers and a projector

- ☐ Document camera

- ☐ Wireless slate

- ☐ Student response system

A laptop cart for student use was shared among the classrooms.

Professional development in technology is challenging because everyone has a unique background that determines individual comfort levels and skill sets. The professional development sessions for the project participants were not specifically tutorials on how to use the equipment. Instead, we focused mainly on curriculum work using the new technology. How might lessons be restructured to take advantage of the technology? Of course, for some teachers it *was* necessary to incorporate information and practice using the technological tools. And so this really was a blended focus in some cases.

During our initial time together, each teacher created a unit of instruction to use with his or her students. Teachers would then teach their new units. Then, at the next professional development session, the teachers would bring with them student artifacts from the units, and we would discuss changes or modifications they thought were needed to make the units more effective. We repeated this cycle several times. I provided direct instruction on new teaching strategies and assessment methods during each session.

The participating teachers were not entirely on their own between face-to-face professional development sessions. Using School Town (http://schooltown.net), a subscription content-management system, each week I would provide them with a new link, idea, or strategy to try. Some weeks, they would use the chat feature of

School Town to discuss the curriculum. Other weeks, they would use the threaded-discussion feature. Using this platform kept everyone connected and communicating.

Coaching days also were part of the schedule, as was time for model lessons and troubleshooting. The team would set a classroom visit schedule, and I would move from room to room, offering support, suggestions, and reflections. If a teacher wanted me to teach a model lesson, we would plan what and when in advance.

This type of professional development is not inexpensive, but it is critical to systemic, ongoing change. In this project, I came in as the outside expert, but in other districts, an instructional coach or a teacher on assignment for technology could undertake my role.

Rethinking Professional Development

IWBs and other technological tools, whether Web 2.0 or hardware/software interfaces, will not transform teaching. A great deal of expensive "stuff" sits idle unless educators—from the building principal to the teacher's aide—are committed to substantive, ongoing learning. Such learning must be aimed not merely at fully using available technology but, more important, employing technological tools to improve students' learning.

The teams in the previous example already were interested in changing how they taught and were committed to learning. Their actions were supported by their school leaders who probably, in the absence of grant funding, would have sought to fund professional development in some other way. But these teachers also were committed to personal learning, not simply attending professional development sessions. This commitment was evident in the ways they used networking to connect to colleagues and to engage in collaborative learning.

As we look to the future, I am convinced that all educators need to be re-energized and re-educated to make the most of new teaching and active-learning opportunities.

Not long ago, I was working on a project with a veteran teacher, and she told me that all of her friends were teasing her because she had become so reinvigorated about teaching. After twenty-five years in the intermediate grades, she was changing how she taught. An interactive whiteboard had been installed in her classroom. She loved the board and its software and could not stop talking about it. She felt completely reborn as a teacher. She explained that she finally had figured out that she does not have to be the source of all knowledge. She can get out of her students' way and turn them loose to learn independently. Finally, she said, teaching is fun again. She can't wait to get to her classroom to explore and to learn. This type of professional rebirth can occur in every classroom.

Many students are more knowledgeable than their teachers when it comes to new technology. Adolescents, in particular, are early adopters. Consequently, students sometimes can take an important role in their teachers' professional development. For example, a middle school technology club made a series of videos for their teachers about common mistakes, problems, and corrective procedures for using IWBs. Making the videos was a learning experience for the students, but the videos themselves—short, funny, and educational all in one—helped teachers become more effective users of the interactive whiteboards in their classrooms.

R&D Teams of the Future

R&D—research and development—is a business concept in origin but applies in all endeavors, especially in the Web 2.0 world of education. In a recent workshop, a participant wanted to know if an audio version of a particular book existed; she wanted the book for one of her students. I posed this question to my Twitter network of some 1,800 people and immediately received a message from the public timeline—an open stream of tweets—with someone offering to check with the publisher. In less than ten minutes, another message came, saying, "We have contacted the publisher, and there is no known version of that book available as an audio book." The next message said, "This is what our company does. We locate books for teachers. Let us know if we can help in the future." I did not have to do the research; the network brought me the answer.

My network is my research and development team. The development aspect enters whenever I want the how-to's. Often, if I want to learn how to use a new technological tool that I have discovered through my network, I request help from the network to see if someone would like to learn with me. Those of us who are interested and available learn together, test out the tool, and then share our experiences with the larger network.

Traditional Resources in New Forms

Professional development for educators needs to change for many reasons. The "sit and get" workshops do not translate into changing practice in the classroom. They are not cost effective, and it is time out of the classrooms away from students. Herding teachers into the cafetorium for the opening day institute does not change instructional practice. In professional development that works, there is a wraparound model in which the information is presented in a variety of ways, the teachers get to practice the strategies, the group reassembles and refines their understanding, and then they serve as coaches and mentors. This has to be systemic and ongoing.

Educators also have to take responsibility for their own personal professional development. I use the Twitter platform for my personal professional development, and my personal learning network is scattered across the globe. The discussion about educational technology continues 24/7, and I tune in when I can. I continue to read books and journals, but I gain a great deal from the short bursts of information delivered to me in 140 characters or less.

New online tools can support professional development. For example, I often teach classes online using the platform Elluminate (www.elluminate.com) or GoToMeeting (www.gotomeeting.com). Adjusting to teaching via webcam and the interactive platform took some getting used to, but after redesigning my presentations, I saw the potential to reach a broader audience. I often lead webinars on selected topics that are offered for free through various partnerships.

Numerous companies are offering subscription-based professional development courses and workshops. I partnered with Knowledge Delivery Systems (www.kdsi.org) to create a video course titled Teaching, Learning and Leading in the Digital Age, offering professional development that does not interfere with teachers' schedules and family demands. PBS TeacherLine (www.pbs.org/teacherline) and Learner.org (www.learner.org) offer similar services.

Many districts are getting into this business themselves by creating online professional development specifically for their staff members. One such district is DeKalb County School System in Georgia. They provide professional development to more than thirteen thousand staff members serving one hundred thousand plus students. The do-it-yourself professional development portal they created allows staff to log in when they can fit it into their schedules. Their success story was featured in the June/July 2010 issue of *Learning & Leading With Technology*.

Professional development is critical to success. It must be personal and collaborative, systematic, and ongoing, changing as the needs of the teachers change. Just as educators need to differentiate instruction for students, so, too, must education leaders differentiate professional learning for teachers. Leaders need to set high expectations, collaborate with teachers to set goals, provide support for professional learning, and follow through to check periodically for continuous professional growth. Ongoing professional dialogue should be the norm. And everyone needs permission to learn, relearn, and learn again.

Looking Forward

Successful teachers in the future will be mashup masters. They will select tools and resources from traditional sources, such as textbooks and classroom learning kits, and mash them up with new resources, including Web 2.0 tools and information, much of it generated through professional networking. Increasingly, textbooks are no longer *the* curriculum, nor are they even a significant part of the curriculum in many schools. Traditional textbooks, in fact, will probably become obsolete as school districts and publishers turn to more interactive digital, software, and Web-based formats for delivering curricular content.

New Approach to Curriculum

I am not suggesting that teachers start writing curricula from scratch. But I do believe that professional thinking and conversations need to shift to what is possible when we all collaborate and share. Leveraging the social media tools discussed in this book can help us connect with one another to create new learning experiences for students. Instead of being isolated in our classrooms, what can we mash up together?

The curriculum of the future will not be a binder filled with lesson plans and worksheets. Nor will it be simply a list of standards with teachers left to their own devices to teach to them, with success measured only by a high-stakes test. In some form, the curriculum of the future will be a hyperlinked collection of resources. Ideally, this new approach to curriculum will be supported by open access to resources that in earlier eras would have been constrained not only by traditional formats but also by restrictive copyrights. The goal, thus, is a core curriculum with optimal flexibility to mash up collateral tools and resources to meet the individualized needs of teachers and students. In essence, this means growing a body of collective knowledge, in effect, creating a wiki of educational possibilities.

To reach this goal, however, we must begin by asking some important questions:

- ☐ What questions or topics (matched to standards) should be addressed in the curriculum?

- ☐ What tools and resources are needed to ensure effective teaching and learning?

- ☐ How should teaching and learning best be organized?

- ☐ How can instructional materials be made most accessible and usable?

- ☐ What collaborations or partnerships would be most productive?

- ☐ What topics or activities should be eliminated because they are obsolete or unproductive?

What I am suggesting is not merely a shift from today's curriculum norm; it is a complete change in thinking. And there is an urgent need to get started wherever this new approach to curriculum does not yet exist.

Take Learning Personally

One of my reasons for writing this book was to help bring curriculum and technology together to create a powerful environment for transformed teaching and learning. Another was to emphasize the importance of a personal commitment to professional growth—the impetus that often leads to dramatic changes in the classroom and positively affects student achievement. Web 2.0 and related tools for professional learning are available in ever-growing numbers and with ever-increasing sophistication. Currently, I am using Twitter for my professional networking. But tomorrow I might be riding Google Wave (http://wave.google.com/help/wave/closed.html)—yes, it's real. The tools will change, but after experiencing the power of using social media for collaborative professional learning, I will always value and stay connected to a network of like-minded educators.

I passionately hope that you will connect with others, select from the many tools I have highlighted, and begin or expand your professional conversations about changing education—whether you are a new teacher or a veteran of the classroom, a curriculum leader or a school administrator. Whatever your role, this is your moment to get involved in this important endeavor.

A Compendium of Web 2.0 Tools and Related Resources

The tools that I have mentioned throughout this book (and a few others) are categorized by topic. The topics are in alphabetical order, and the tools within the categories also are alphabetical. This compendium is intended as a handy summary resource, not a comprehensive guide. Of course, many of the tools are multifunctional. For example, Google Docs also can be used as a wiki. I have placed the tools in the category in which they are most often used. I have concentrated on software and Internet-based tools, rather than hardware—with a couple of exceptions.

Many tools, of course, are evolving: features change; functionalities are added. Sometimes tools become wholly obsolete and are discarded. New tools emerge. Networking is a way to stay abreast of changes. Another way to stay current is to subscribe to Kathy Schrock's Guide for Educators on the Discovery Education website (http://school.discoveryeducation.com/schrockguide/sos.html). Kathy is a leader in the Web 2.0 revolution.

Also, readers should feel free to follow me on Twitter. I am constantly tweeting about the sites I am currently using, what is working, and what is not working. My Twitter name is "megormi."

Blogs and Blogging

Blogging allows students to post texts and comment on other people's writing, to discuss or brainstorm topics, and to create a collection of frequently asked questions (FAQs). Full-size blog sites are complemented by micro-blogging sites that limit the number of words or characters in a text entry.

Blogger

Blogger (www.blogger.com) is a blog site owned by Google. It is quick and easy to set up but is supported by advertisements that appear on the blog pages.

Class Blogmeister

Class Blogmeister (http://classblogmeister.com) is a free blog engine created by David Warlick, founder of the Landmark Project.

Google Wave

Google Wave (http://wave.google.com/about.html) is a collaborative space enabling people who share a wave to share, edit, publish, and create mashups of text, pictures, maps, documents, videos, and more. A wave is live, making it possible for participants to interact in real time.

Plurk

Plurk (www.plurk.com) is a popular micro-blogging site with posts viewed in a timeline.

Twitter

Twitter (http://twitter.com) is a micro-blogging site; each post is limited to 140 characters or fewer. A number of Twitter companion sites include:

- ☐ Mr. Tweet (http://mrtweet.com)

- ☐ Seesmic Desktop (http://seesmic.com)

- ☐ SnapTweet (http://snaptweet.com)

- ☐ TweetDeck (http://tweetdeck.com/beta)

- ☐ Twitter4Teachers wiki (http://twitter4teachers.pbworks. com)

☐ TwitPic (http://twitpic.com)

☐ WeFollow (http://wefollow.com)

Calendars

There are many online solutions for calendar management. Online calendars offer the flexibility of sharing different layers of your life with different people. Moving your calendar online gives greater access to the information when and where you need it.

Google Calendar

Google Calendar (www.google.com/calendar) is a color-coded calendar with various layers for different purposes. Each layer can be made either public or private.

iCal

iCal (www.apple.com/support/ical) is an Apple application with the ability to share calendars with other iCal users.

Cell Phones

We need to consider the potential of cell phones as teaching and learning tools. They offer the possibility of one-to-one computing in the classroom.

Poll Everywhere

Poll Everywhere (www.polleverywhere.com) enables data collection through cell phone texting. There is a limit of thirty responses per poll in the free version.

TextTheMob

TextTheMob (http://textthemob.com) allows one hundred people to respond to a poll using the free version. Users set up polls, and respondents text in their answers.

Content Management

Content management systems allow teachers to organize course material in an online environment. These systems allow students

to pick up assignments, turn in assignments, chat, and publish artifacts to the online gallery.

Joomla!

Joomla! (www.joomla.org) is open-source software for content
management, similar to Moodle (see next).

Moodle

Moodle (http://moodle.org) is hosted software that creates a virtual
classroom environment. Many features can be enabled, including
discussions, wikis, file sharing, and uploading of media.

School Town

School Town (http://schooltown.net) is a subscription content-
management system with many features that are easy to navigate.

Conversion Sites

A number of websites provide the ability to convert online videos
for offline viewing. In addition, certain software also can convert files into various formats. I have focused on the online sites
because many people in schools have limited privileges to install
software. Conversion can allow students and teachers to mash up
content in a variety of ways, for instance, using video or audio
clips in PowerPoint presentations.

All2Convert

All2Convert (www.all2convert.com) is a simple conversion site
with output in a variety of file formats.

Convert Direct

Convert Direct (www.convertdirect.com) offers a wide range of
file formats from which to select.

Format Factory

Format Factory (www.formatoz.com) offers downloadable software.

KeepVid

KeepVid (http://keepvid.com) provides a button that can be added to the user's computer toolbar.

Media Converter

Media Converter (www.mediaconverter.org) provides a free interface, but there is a limit of five daily downloads and conversions. Other paid options are available.

Movavi

Movavi (www.movavi.com) software is offered for a fee, but the site also has a limited, five-per-day URL conversion feature.

WinFF

WinFF (http://winff.org/html_new) can convert videos (several at once) quickly and easily. The downloadable software is free.

Zamzar

Zamzar (www.zamzar.com) sends the converted file to your email to download.

Copyright

It is very important to model ethical behavior in use of online resources. Students need to understand that there are copyright limits, and the projects that they create should align to these guidelines.

Copyright Laws

An online manuscript, *K–12 Copyright Laws: Primer for Teachers* (www.edu-cyberpg.com/Teachers/copyrightlaw.html), provides basic do's and don'ts for educators.

Creative Commons

Creative Commons (http://creativecommons.org) is a nonprofit organization that increases sharing and improves collaboration by giving users permission to use selected images, video clips, audio clips, and other media.

Digital Journals

Current professional reading can be found in a number of online journals and magazines. Examples include:

- ☐ *eSchool News* (www.eschoolnews.com)

- ☐ *International Journal of Emerging Technologies in Learning* (iJET) (www.online-journals.org/i-jet)

- ☐ *Learning Solutions Magazine* (www.learningsolutionsmag. com)

Ebook Readers

The category of ebook readers covers a number of name-brand devices that make it possible to read a book that has been downloaded or purchased. This is an emerging market as more ebook readers are released and more and more books are becoming available digitally. Many textbook manufacturers are racing to provide their books electronically.

iPad

Reading books digitally is just one of thousands of potential uses for the iPad.

Kindle

The Kindle is the reader that is tied to Amazon. This device allows you to download books on the fly, without synching to a computer.

Nook

The nook is Barnes & Noble's offering in the ebook reader market.

Sony Reader

The Sony Reader has the flexibility to download books from the Sony site or from some public libraries. If the book is checked out from the public library, it is removed electronically from the ebook reader at the end of the lending period.

Email

Email allows teachers to efficiently communicate with their students, other staff members, and parents. Many school districts are beginning to offer email addresses to students, allowing them to hand in assignments electronically and to contact teachers as needed.

Gmail

Gmail (http://mail.google.com) is Google's email feature. The conversations are organized differently than traditional emails; conversations that have the same subject line are grouped together.

Outlook Webmail

Many districts still use Microsoft Outlook to manage their email. Most districts have their email available on the Web, accessible through the school website.

Zoho Mail

Zoho Mail (http://mail.zoho.com) is an online mail solution powered by Zoho and can be accessed from any computer or cell phone connected to the Internet. (See also, Zoho in the Productivity and Professional Development category.)

Image Collections

There are countless image collections available on the Internet. In this book, we are just highlighting a few. All images should be used appropriately, respecting copyright guidelines. Remember, when searching for images, never do the search in front of a class; screen and preselect the images first.

Flickr

Flickr (www.flickr.com) is one of the largest databases for images and videos.

Library of Congress

The Library of Congress (www.loc.gov/index.html) holds and makes available photographic images from the Civil War era to the present. Other images and documents go back even further.

National Archives

National Archives (www.archives.gov) is a trove of still photos, as well as audio and video clips of historic events, lesson plans, and other resources.

Image Manipulation

Images can be manipulated on various websites. Most of these sites are not appropriate to use with students but are a great way for teachers to generate images for vocabulary work and graphics for websites.

Add Letters

Add Letters (www.addletters.com) generates your name on various signs.

BeFunky

BeFunky (www.befunky.com) allows you to apply effects to digital photos.

Big Huge Labs

Big Huge Labs (http://bighugelabs.com) offers several tools to manipulate photos.

FACEinHOLE.com

FACEinHOLE.com (www.faceinhole.com) allows you to select a new body on which to place your face.

Fun Photo Box

Fun Photo Box (http://funphotobox.com) offers several effects to create funny photos.

ImageChef

ImageChef (www.imagechef.com) generates an image from available templates.

JibJab

JibJab (http://sendables.jibjab.com) allows you to create your own JibJab.

Loonapix

Loonapix (www.loonapix.com) allows you to put your face on various templates.

MagMyPic

MagMyPic (www.magmypic.com) allows you to create fun magazine covers.

MushyGushy

MushyGushy (www.mushygushy.com) allows you to put your face into various animated scenes.

myFrame.us

myFrame.us (http://myframe.us) allows you to frame your pictures for free.

My Movie Moment

My Movie Moment (http://mymoviemoment.com) allows you to add an image to a movie clip.

Photo505

Photo505 (www.photo505.com) offers effects to manipulate photos.

PhotoFunia

PhotoFunia (http://photofunia.com) allows you to put your face on Mount Rushmore and more.

PicArtia

PicArtia (www.makeuseof.com/dir/picartia) allows you to create photo mosaics.

Pimp the Face

At Pimp the Face (www.pimptheface.com), you can change or create a face.

Space Your Face

Space Your Face (http://spaceyourface.nasa.gov) allows you to put your face on a dancing astronaut.

Maps and Mapping

There are many sites for simply viewing maps online. Other sites allow you to manipulate the map and offer software that can be downloaded to allow for a more sophisticated analysis of a geographic area.

Google Earth

Google Earth (http://earth.google.com) is free software from Google that enables users to "fly" virtually anywhere in the world. Tours can be created or downloaded from the Internet. Layers provide various types of information, including traffic, weather, important sites, images, and so on.

Google Maps

Google Maps (http://maps.google.com) is an online resource where users can search by address, get directions, and find places of interest.

Miscellaneous

This section includes those tools that do not fit directly in the groups provided. These resources have specific purposes and uses and should be part of every digital-rich classroom.

Flip

Flip (www.theflip.com/en-us) video cameras are inexpensive (ranging from $130 to $250) and easy to use. The necessary software comes preloaded on the camera.

Wolfram Alpha

Wolfram Alpha (www.wolframalpha.com) is a computational knowledge engine that contains trillions of pieces of data.

Modeling

Software can be downloaded enabling students to create 3-D models for a wide variety of projects. Creating a 3-D model helps the student better visualize the details and allows for deeper comprehension.

Google Building Maker

Google Building Maker (http://sketchup.google.com/3dwh/buildingmaker.html) is a software download that guides the user through the process of creating buildings, which then can be inserted into Google Earth.

Google SketchUp

Google SketchUp (http://sketchup.google.com/download) is 3-D modeling software that includes a link to an online warehouse of 3-D objects that can be imported and resized for various projects.

Multimedia Creation

Multimedia creation is exploding on the Internet, with new tools popping up all the time. Many of these sites are appropriate to use with students, but make sure you preview them, specifically looking at the gallery, if there is one.

Glogster

Glogster (www.glogster.com) is a website that allows users to mash up various media, tying together video, audio, still images, text, animations, and graphics. The products are referred to as Glogs.

VoiceThread

VoiceThread (http://voicethread.com) is a free online multimedia-creation website that allows users to upload video, record audio, add still images, and create a digital story by mashing all of the elements together.

Podcasting

Podcasting refers to an audio file that has been recorded for playback on a computer, an iPod, an iPad, or an mp3 player. The largest collection of podcasts is found at Apple's iTunes Store.

Audacity

Audacity (http://audacity.sourceforge.net) is free, open-source software that can be downloaded and installed to create podcasts.

GarageBand

GarageBand (www.apple.com/ilife/garageband) is a powerful Mac app to create podcasts, but it is not available for PCs.

iTunes Store

To access the iTunes Store, you need to download the iTunes software, which is compatible with both Mac and PC operating systems. The iTunes Store (www.apple.com/itunes) is searchable and a source for subscribing to existing podcasts. Podcasts that users create also can be uploaded to their iTunes playlist and shared with others or downloaded to listening devices.

iTunes U

iTunes U (www.apple.com/education/itunes-u) is an educational application using the popular Apple iTunes platform; it offers a growing collection of educational podcasts on many topics.

Productivity and Professional Development

In the past, you needed to purchase software to do things like word processing and creating presentations and spreadsheets.

Today, there are many free options that include websites and software that can be downloaded.

Google Apps Education Edition

Google Apps Education Edition (www.google.com/a/help/intl/en/edu/index.html) is a broad, school-oriented website especially created for education. Google Apps Education Edition offers numerous features, from backing up data to 24/7 access without compromising the school network.

Google Docs

Google Docs (http://docs.google.com) is a wide-ranging collection of tools that allows users to create documents, spreadsheets, presentations, and forms. This online resource is powerful, and almost all related applications are free.

GoToMeeting

GoToMeeting (www.gotomeeting.com) is a website-based service that provides an online meeting/in-service platform.

OpenOffice.org

OpenOffice.org (www.openoffice.org) is an open-source productivity suite that can be downloaded. Although not as feature-rich as Microsoft Office, the software is powerful and works well. Documents can be saved in a variety of formats.

Zoho

Zoho (www.zoho.com) is an online productivity solution. This free service includes word processing, spreadsheets, presentations, calendars, wikis, discussions, contact management solutions, and much more.

RSS Readers

RSS stands for "really simple syndication." What it means is that you can subscribe to a blog or a website and when its content is updated, it is pushed to your reader.

Bloglines

Bloglines (www.bloglines.com) is my preferred RSS reader. Once subscribed to a feed, Bloglines makes it easy to review fresh content.

Google Reader

Google Reader (www.google.com/reader) is Google's solution to organizing the online content that you subscribe to. The nice thing about Google Reader is that your feeds can appear on your iGoogle page.

NewsGator

NewsGator (www.newsgator.com) offers a suite of RSS readers and has been adopted by many businesses trying to make sense of how to market in a social networking environment.

Screencasting

Screencasting is when a user records while navigating the Web. The software picks up every move online as well as the user's voice, in essence creating a movie of the process. Screencasting can be an effective way to introduce new software or processes to students.

Camtasia Studio

Camtasia Studio (www.techsmith.com/camtasia.asp) is robust screencasting software that can be purchased. It has many output options and no limit on the length of the screencast.

Jing

Jing (www.jingproject.com) is free "webcasting" software from the makers of Camtasia Studio, but the screencasts are limited to five minutes in length.

Social Networking

Social networking websites enable people to connect online. Users of social networking run the gamut from preschoolers to online grandmas.

Classroom 2.0

Classroom 2.0 (www.classroom20.com), created on the Ning (see page 128) platform, is a social network adapted for educators' professional networking.

Delicious

Delicious (http://delicious.com) is a social network about bookmarks. After creating a free account, bookmarks can then be saved and left public or made private.

Facebook

Facebook (www.facebook.com) is currently the fastest growing social networking site. It was started for the college set, slipped to high schoolers at first by invitation only, and then in the fall of 2006 was opened to anyone worldwide.

LibraryThing

LibraryThing (www.librarything.com) allows registered members to create their own virtual bookshelves. After a user enters a title of a book, the site imports information about the book and an image of the book cover from Amazon.com.

Livemocha

Livemocha (www.livemocha.com) is a social network for learning another language while also helping someone learn your native language. Users trade time helping and learning, and all of the lessons and assessments by native speakers are free.

MySpace

MySpace (www.myspace.com) has roots in garage bands trying to establish a following. The popularity of this site is declining with Facebook's rising dominance in social networking.

Ning

Ning (www.ning.com) is a free platform that enables users to create their own social networks. Ning makes setup and management seamless with a variety of templates.

Shelfari

Shelfari (www.shelfari.com), like LibraryThing, is a social networking site about books. Shelfari also lets the user create a widget—a small piece of software that can be added to a website for added functionality—to showcase books and show them on the user's blog.

Student Response Systems

Student response systems are small handheld devices that allow students to enter information, which is then displayed on a screen. Student responses are collected and saved on the teacher's computer. The software that comes with the student response system allows the teacher to manipulate the data and look for trends.

ActiVote

ActiVote (www.prometheanworld.com/server.php?show=nav.16) is the student response system produced by Promethean, a company that also sells the Promethean Interactive Whiteboard.

CPSPulse

One of the features of the CPSPulse by eInstruction (www.einstruction.com/products/assessment/index.html) is the ability to work offline, meaning that the students can work at their own pace. CPSPulse also interfaces with ExamView, a bank of exam questions that is used by many textbook companies.

Qwizdom

Qwizdom by Qwizdom Incorporated (www.qwizdom.com) can be used for formative assessments and online reporting of data. The software that comes with Qwizdom simplifies recordkeeping for the teacher.

ResponseCards

ResponseCards by Turning Technologies (www.turningtechnologies
.com) are small devices that are easy to store. Most of the systems
have a range of two hundred to four hundred feet.

Video and Audio

There are many online sources for video and audio. Throughout the
book, I have highlighted a number of those resources. In the ever-
changing Web 2.0 world, more and more sites are popping up.

Adobe Premiere Elements

Adobe Premiere Elements (www.adobe.com/ap/products
/premiereel) is software that can be purchased for approximately
$60 and is useful for more complex video-editing projects. This
software allows for multiple layers of audio, thus resulting in a
more professional video product.

BubbleJoy

BubbleJoy (www.bubblejoy.com) adds frames to video clips to
make clever video cards that can be emailed.

Cameroid

Cameroid (www.cameroid.com) creates a graphic (jpg format) to
be saved or emailed. Backgrounds and frames of all sorts are available. The image generator can be used with a webcam to incorporate video.

Discovery Streaming

Discovery Streaming (http://streaming.discoveryeducation.com),
formerly United Streaming, is a subscription website filled with
thousands of downloadable educational videos. Other resources
include lesson plans, video quizzes, still images, songs, and sound
effects.

Freeplay Music

Freeplay Music (http://freeplaymusic.com) allows artists to submit music and sound effects. While visiting the site, you can search for different genres of music and listen to short clips.

iDVD

iDVD (www.apple.com/ilife/idvd) is only available on Apple computers. It seamlessly integrates iMovie into DVD production.

iMovie

iMovie (www.apple.com/ilife/imovie) is video-editing software that can create very sophisticated video productions. It is only available on Apple computers.

iTunes

iTunes (www.apple.com/itunes) is software that can be downloaded for free and runs on both Macs and PCs. Users can create a library of songs, podcasts, and videos and purchase all of these through the iTunes Store.

Library of Congress

See listing in Image Collections category.

Movie Maker

Movie Maker (www.microsoft.com/windowsxp/downloads/updates/moviemaker2.mspx) is software that comes preloaded on every PC that is running Windows XP and above. For those people running Windows 7, it is free to download. This software can be used for video-editing projects.

National Archives

See listing in Image Collections category.

Royalty Free Music.com

At Royalty Free Music.com (www.royaltyfreemusic.com/free-music-resources.html) artists have uploaded music that can be previewed and downloaded.

SchoolTube.com

SchoolTube.com (www.schooltube.com) partners with schools to serve as a portal for videos created by students.

TeacherTube

TeacherTube (http://teachertube.com) is an education-friendly uploading site, similar to but slower than YouTube.

Ustream

Ustream (www.ustream.tv) is a live video-broadcasting platform.

YouTube

YouTube (www.youtube.com) is the largest Internet database of video clips.

Voice Over IP

Voice (or video) over Internet Protocol is software that uses an Internet connection to allow communication among people who have voice over IP client software.

Google Voice

Google Voice (www.google.com/voice) allows users to select a Google phone number and up to five numbers to which to forward calls. Users can then use this Google number instead of sharing a cell phone or home phone number. It also features voicemail and the option to have messages transcribed to text.

Skype

Skype (http://skype.com) is free, downloadable software that enables free voice and video calls from computer to computer anywhere in the world. Additional features include chat, desktop sharing, and other add-ons. A fee is charged for calls to landlines and cell phones.

Website Creation

In the past, special software was needed to create a website. Mastery of various computer languages such as HTML was necessary and you had to pay for Web hosting services. Today, there are online solutions that are template based and can be housed for free.

Google Sites

Google Sites (http://sites.google.com) provides free, online website hosting and creation tools. Template-driven functions make it easy for beginners.

Wikis

Wikis are websites that enable their members to get into the same virtual space. The person who created the wiki controls it. Wikis can be open or shared within a defined group. A wiki needs to be hosted online, and there are many choices. The most popular host sites are Wikispaces and PBworks, both listed below.

PBworks

PBworks (http://PBworks.com) offers free wiki sites to educators. Template backgrounds facilitate personalizing the look of a user's wiki.

Wikipedia

Wikipedia (www.wikipedia.org) is the largest of the wikis and provides an online, user-created encyclopedia that has become a first go-to resource for many people. Researchers should beware, however, that due to Wikipedia's very nature of being user-created and edited, facts should always be verified from another source.

Wikispaces

Wikispaces (www.wikispaces.com) is committed to education and currently offers free wikis to educators.

Words and Vocabulary

The following are some of the sites that I like to use when working with words. Adding the visual element to vocabulary words can help students to make connections.

Add Letters

Add Letters (www.addletters.com) is a graphic-generating website based on text entered by the user, similar to ImageChef.

ImageChef

ImageChef (www.imagechef.com) is one of many online custom-graphics generators. The "Word Mosaic" feature is similar in some aspects to Wordle.

Wordle

Wordle (www.wordle.net/create) is a tag-cloud generator. Wordle creates tag clouds from any text that is typed into the site. The words that are used more often appear larger.

References and Resources

Alexander, S., & Henderson-Rosser, A. (2010, June/July). Do-it-yourself professional development. *Learning & Leading with Technology, 37*(8), 24–27.

Anderson, C. (2006). *The long tail: Why the future of business is selling less of more.* New York: Hyperion.

Catone, J. (2009, August 17). Digital textbooks: 3 reasons students aren't ready. Accessed at http://mashable.com/2009/08/17/digital-textbooks on June 1, 2010.

Christensen, C. M. (2008). *Disrupting class: How disruptive innovation will change the way the world learns.* New York: McGraw-Hill Companies.

Churches, A. (2009). Bloom's Digital Taxonomy: It's not about the tools; it's using the tools to facilitate learning. Accessed at http://edorigami.wikispaces.com/file/view/bloom%27s+Digital+taxonomy+v3.01.pdf on May 21, 2010.

Dewey, J. (1938). *Experience and education.* New York: Macmillan.

DuFour, R., Eaker, R., & DuFour, R. (Eds.). (2005). *On common ground: The power of professional learning communities.* Bloomington, IN: Solution Tree Press (formerly National Educational Service).

Facebook. (2009). Facebook Press Room. Accessed at www.facebook.com/press on January 20, 2010.

Gee, J. P. (2003). *What video games have to teach us about learning and literacy.* New York: Palgrave Macmillan.

Gladwell, M. (2002). *The tipping point: How little things can make a big difference.* New York: Little, Brown and Company.

Godin, S. (2008). *Tribes: We need you to lead us.* New York: Penguin Books.

Hattie, J., & Timperley, H. (2007). The power of feedback. *Review of Educational Research, 77*(1), 81–112.

Helft, M., & Richtel, M. (2006, October 10). Venture firm shares a YouTube jackpot. *New York Times.* Accessed at www.nytimes.com/2006/10/10/technology/10payday.html on June 1, 2010.

Hyerle, D. (1996). *Visual tools for constructing knowledge.* Alexandria, VA: Association for Supervision and Curriculum Development.

International Society for Technology in Education. (2000). *National educational technology standards for students.* Eugene, OR: Author.

Israel, S. (2009). *Twitterville.* New York: Penguin Group.

Jensen, E. (1998). *Teaching with the brain in mind.* Alexandria, VA: Association for Supervision and Curriculum Development.

Johnson, S. (2009, June 15). How Twitter will change the way we live (in 140 characters or less). *Time, 173*(23), 32–37.

Jukes, I., McCain, T., & Crockett, L. (2010). *Understanding the digital generation: Teaching and learning in the new digital landscape.* Thousand Oaks, CA: Corwin Press.

Kotter, J. P. (2008). *A sense of urgency.* Boston: Harvard Business Press.

LeDoux, J. (1994). Emotion, memory, and the brain. *Scientific American, 270*(6), 50–57.

Marzano, R. J. (2008). *Getting serious about school reform: Three critical commitments.* Bloomington, IN: Marzano Research Laboratory.

Marzano, R. J., & Pickering, D. J. (2005). *Building academic vocabulary: Teacher's manual.* Alexandria, VA: Association for Supervision and Curriculum Development.

Marzano, R. J., Pickering, D. J., & Pollock, J. E. (2001). *Classroom instruction that works: Research-based strategies for increasing student achievement.* Alexandria, VA: Association for Supervision and Curriculum Development.

Marzano, R. J., & Waters, T. (in press). *From the boardroom to the classroom: District leadership that works.* Alexandria, VA: Association for Supervision and Curriculum Development.

Marzano Research Laboratory. (2009). *Evaluation study of the effects of Promethean ActivClassroom on student achievement.* Accessed at www.marzanoresearch.com/documents/Preliminary%20 Report%20on%20ActivClassroom.pdf on September 14, 2009.

Ohanian, S. (1988). On stir-and-serve recipes for teaching. In K. Ryan & J. M. Cooper (Eds.), *Kaleidoscope: Readings in education* (pp. 56–61). Boston: Allyn & Bacon.

Ormiston, M. J. (2004). *Conquering infoclutter: Timesaving technology solutions for teachers* (Vol. 1). Thousand Oaks, CA: Corwin Press.

Ormiston, M., & Standley, M. (2003). *Digital storytelling with PowerPoint* (Vol. 1). Eugene, OR: Visions Technology in Education.

Pink, D. (2005). *A whole new mind: Why right brainers will rule the future.* New York: Penguin Books.

Pitler, H., Hubbell, E. R., Kuhn, M., & Malenoski, K. (2007). *Using technology with classroom instruction that works.* Alexandria, VA: Association for Supervision and Curriculum Development.

Prensky, M. (2001). *Digital game-based learning.* New York: McGraw-Hill.

Rideout, V., Foehr, U., & Roberts, D. (2010). *Generation M: Media in the Lives of 8- to 18-year-olds.* Kaiser Family Foundation. Accessed at www.kff.org/entmedia/upload/Generation-M-Media-in-the-Lives-of-8-18-Year-olds-Report.pdf on May 21, 2010.

Robinson, K. (2009). *The element: How finding your passion changes everything.* New York: Penguin Books.

Rumberger, R. (2004). Why students drop out of school. In G. Orfield (Ed.), *Dropouts in America: Confronting the graduation rate crisis* (pp. 131–155). Cambridge, MA: Harvard Education Press. Accessed at http://educatingthechildren.com/Dropout-Epidemic.html on June 8, 2010.

Schank, R. (2002). *Designing world-class e-learning: How IBM, GE, Harvard Business School, & Columbia University are succeeding at e-learning.* New York: McGraw-Hill.

Schonfeld, E. (2009). Facebook is now the fourth largest site in the world. Accessed at http://techcrunch.com/2009/08/04/facebook-is-now-the-fourth-largest-site-in-the-world on June 1, 2010.

Shkolnikova, S. (2008). Online "open" textbooks save students cash. *USA TODAY.* Accessed at www.usatoday.com/news/

education/2008–07–09-open-textbooks_N.htm on May 13, 2010.

Small, G., & Vorgan, G. (2008). *iBrain: Surviving the technological alteration of the modern mind.* New York: HarperCollins.

Tapscott, D. (2009). *Grown up digital: How the net generation is changing your world.* New York: McGraw-Hill.

Tapscott, D., & Williams, A. (2006). *Wikinomics: How mass collaboration changes everything.* New York: Penguin Books.

Tomlinson, C. A. (1999a). *Differentiation in practice: A resources guide for differentiating curriculum.* Alexandria, VA: Association for Supervision and Curriculum Development.

Tomlinson, C. A. (1999b). *The differentiated classroom: Responding to the needs of all learners.* Alexandria, VA: Association for Supervision and Curriculum Development.

Tomlinson, C. A. (2001). *How to differentiate instruction in mixed-ability classrooms.* Alexandria, VA: Association for Supervision and Curriculum Development.

Willingham, D. (2009). *Why don't students like school? A cognitive scientist answers questions about how the mind works and what it means for the classroom.* San Francisco: Jossey-Bass.

Wolfe, P. (2001). *Brain matters: Translating research into classroom practice.* Alexandria, VA: Association for Supervision and Curriculum Development.

Index

C

essential classroom components
  policies needed, 75–76
  tools needed, 77–84
  vision and collaboration,
    76–77
integrating standards with,
  43–45
integration in classroom, 3
policies
  changes needed in, 15–17
  necessity of, 75–76
professional development and,
  98–100
standards for, 42
student knowledge of, 9–13
writing instruction and, 55–58
television for current students, 11
textbooks
  curriculum versus, 61
  digital textbooks, 65–67
text messaging, educational usage
  of, 25–26. *See also* cell phone
  usage
TextTheMob, 115
Tomlinson, Carol, 3, 16, 29, 90, 93
tools. *See also* websites
  in active-learning case study,
    92–93
  for audio and video, 129–131
  for blogging, 113–115
  for calendars, 115
  cell phones, 115
  for collaboration, 124–125
  for content management,
    115–116
  copyright issues, 117–118
  desirable classroom
    components, 85–86
  ebook readers, 118–119
  for email, 119
  essential classroom components,
    77–84
    document camera, 82–83

  interactive whiteboard, 80–81
  multifunction speakers,
    81–82
  network access, 83–84
  student laptop, 79–80
  student response systems, 83
  teacher laptop, 78–79
  voice amplification system,
    82
  for file conversion, 116–117
  image collections, 119–120
  for image manipulation,
    120–122
  for maps, 122
  for modeling, 123
  for multimedia creation,
    123–124
  for networking, 100–103
  for podcasts, 124
  for screencasting, 126
  social networking sites, 126–128
  student response systems,
    128–129
  technology as, 58
  for vocabulary development,
    133
  wikis, 43–44, 57–58, 132–133
transitions for still images, 51
Tribes (Godin), 90
TurningPoint Audience Response
  System, 23
TweetDeck, 103, 114
TwitPic, 103, 115
Twitter, 99, 101–103, 113–115
Twitter4Teachers, 102, 114

U

Ustream, 99, 131

V

video games for current students,
  11–12
videos

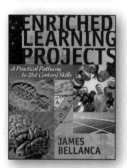

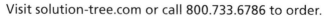